10-19-88

Wood Finishing
and Refinishing

Also by Alan Hall

The Wild Food Trailguide

Alan Hall
James Heard

Wood
Finishing and
Refinishing

Holt, Rinehart and Winston
New York

First published in January 1982 by Holt,
Rinehart and Winston,
383 Madison Avenue, New York, New York 10017.
Published simultaneously in Canada by Holt, Rinehart
and Winston of Canada, Limited.

Library of Congress Cataloging in Publication Data
Hall, Alan, 1945–
Wood finishing and refinishing.
Includes index.
1. Wood finishing. 2. Furniture finishing.
I. Heard, James. II. Title.
TT325.H29   684.1′043   81-4708   AACR2
ISBN Hardbound: 0–03–018856–3
ISBN Paperback: 0–03–018861–X (An Owl Book)

First Edition

Designer: Amy Hill
Printed in the United States of America
10   9   8   7   6   5   4   3   2   1

Contents

Foreword

When I first met Jim Heard in 1967, he was running an antique shop on New York's Lower East Side. What set that antique shop apart from others in a neighborhood where, at that time, antique stores were more common than mosquitos in New Jersey, was that all the things for sale glowed with the rich luster of fine finishes. Whether it was a factory-produced round oak table made around the turn of the century or a handcrafted cherry gentleman's chest built in the early 1800s, whether it had the brassy gloss of a piano or the soft warmth of an old pine kitchen cabinet, the furniture in Heard's store had obviously been touched by hands that respected wood and knew how to make it look its very best.

For the next several years I began spending more and more time in Jim Heard's workshop, and my first impression was confirmed again and again. He had behind him nearly twenty years of experience working with wood and furniture. And he had mastered his craft. He is a precise and uncompromising craftsman who will not settle for anything short of perfection. "I just can't accept a second-to-best finish," he once told me.

It is that background that is the basis for this book. Jim Heard and I have worked to put down as much of what he has learned as possible. The result is a book that we hope will be as informative to the professional finisher as it is to the inexperienced amateur embarking on his first project. We have tried to organize this information in a way that presents what is really a broad and complex subject in a simple, step-by-step manner. And we have attempted to do that without compromising detail.

The chapters are arranged to cover the major operations involved in wood finishing—from removing old finishes and making minor repairs to the final rubbing and polishing. Our intention was to produce a book that contains all the information essential to the finest finishes. It will also help the reader acquire basic skills and, at the same time, find his own way to the creative decisions that make the pursuit of a craft thoroughly engrossing.

In that sense, this is not a how-to book. Rather, it is a book that we hope will act as a road map to show others how to bring the full beauty of wood into the light of day.

Alan Hall

1

The Basics of Wood Finishing

Wood is one of the most beautiful and satisfying materials used by man. It is strong and light, easily worked, and stands beside metals as a material that has shaped the very existence of mankind. For millennia it has touched virtually every phase of life. Civilizations have risen and fallen based on its availability. Wood has provided fuel, housing boats and vehicles, utensils and furniture.

Beyond its utilitarian aspects, wood is a thing of great beauty. It comes in infinite combinations of color, texture, and grain pattern. Just as the wood of no two kinds of trees is identical, no two pieces of wood are the same. The history of every tree is written in its grain. Each part is distinctly different—section by section, board by board. Even the way wood is cut from the log can expose surprising variation. Oak cut one way is a straight-grained wood; cut in the manner sawyers call "quarter cutting," is displays startling bands of light color that run across the grain.

Yet wood simply cut from a log is nothing more than lumber. A rough board is dull and nondescript; sometimes it is even difficult to identify the kind of wood. When wood is smoothed, the grain pattern becomes evident. But it is not until a finish of some kind is applied that wood achieves its fullest expression. In the same manner that a gemstone is little more than a rock with potential until it is ground and polished, so too must wood be sanded and finished. Only then will it capture light like a gemstone and throw it back in refractive waves that make the grain seem to shift and move, that create the illusion of depth instead of a flat surface.

It is with furniture that wood finishing has transcended the practical aspect of protecting the wood and become an art. Finishers have learned to manipulate the intrinsic properties of fine wood to enhance the natural beauty that lurks beneath its surface. By using stains, filling the pores of the wood, and applying clear finishes overall, they are able to even out natural variations, match individual pieces, and allow the wood to express itself in a manner that suits their taste.

The finish is as much a part of furniture as the wood from which it is made and the craftsmanship with which that wood was assembled. An unfinished Chippendale chair or a fine Hepplewhite chest would have more kinship to the inexpensive pine sold in unfinished-furniture stores than those impressive examples found in museums. That, however, is not to say that all wood or furniture deserves the painstaking application of a fine finish. Some furniture is simply utilitarian and some wood is nondescript. For that reason, many pieces were made to be painted. And many finishers have applied their art to making one wood look like another more valuable one or to obscuring the wood completely with colored lacquers and enamels. Many may disagree with their original decision—some early pine kitchen furniture, for instance, looks fine with a clear finish—but in just as many cases, the decision of the furniture maker was beyond reproach.

The effect of clear finishes is the same as wetting the wood. They form a refractive coating. And, like water, they darken the wood somewhat. In fact, the best way to see what a finish will look like on a piece of wood is to rub a spot with a wet finger. The refractivity and reflectivity of the finish can be varied by buffing the finish to a high polish or rubbing it to satiny softness but the wetting effect of applying any clear material to the wood is still the same.

In that sense, there is no such thing as a *natural* finish. The only time wood is natural is when it has no finish at all— a fencepost is natural and so is a barn beam. As soon as anything is applied to the wood, the color and the texture change. Short of not applying any finish at all, the closest finished wood can come to "natural" is the application of a clear coating without any staining or filling. And that is fine. Indeed, some woods like walnut or mahogany, cherry or rosewood can be so impressive in their own right that staining and filling may be an overembellishment. On the other hand, walnut sometimes has prominent white streaks in the heartwood. The visual effect of a piece of walnut furniture is enhanced if these streaks are stained to match the rich brown of the adjoining wood.

Judging a Finish

How much a finisher does to change the appearance of the wood in the interest of better expressing its intrinsic beauty is a matter of personal preference. Still, there are some things that a finish should not do. A properly applied finish should never detract from the appearance of the wood or obscure it. Stain should leave a surface coloration that looks natural even though it may be somewhat better than reality, rather like movies in which the grass is greener than any grass could ever be. The stain should also leave the wood clear and visible: improperly applied stain will leave a piece that is blotchy or muddy-looking, no matter how carefully the later finish coats are applied.

A good finish depends on care at each step. If a piece has

not been sanded to absolute smoothness before staining, it will remain rough and dull-looking no matter how much effort is put into applying the final coats of finish. Improper sealing after staining will permit the stain to bleed into the finish coats, obscuring the grain and blurring the finish. Filler left on the surface and not packed into the pores of the wood will have a similar effect. And careless use of colored spray lacquers—which, if used skillfully, can hide defects and improve the appearance of inexpensive woods—will make a piece appear to have been painted.

In the final analysis, a good finish lets the inherent features of the wood show through. The figure of the wood should be clear and distinct, every pore and crevice of the grain magnified and clearly visible from across a room. Such finishes, however, are difficult to find. The mass-produced furniture sold in stores most commonly has a sprayed-on lacquer finish. Stain is usually mixed with the first coat. Although the coats are few, the wood may be somewhat obscured. Lacquer can, of course, be used to make a very fine finish, but such finishes are found only on the most expensively crafted furniture. In defense of industrial finishing, it must be said that furniture would be prohibitively costly without it. In fact, about the only place to see what a truly fine finish looks like is the stores that sell extremely fine furniture or in museums. And the least costly way to own furniture with such fine finishes is to put them on yourself.

Applying Fine Finishes

Finishing wood requires a number of skills. But none of them are so difficult that they require years of training to acquire, although they may take years to master. Finishes superior to those on much of the mass-produced furniture can be applied by the inexperienced amateur. With practice, it is possible to become very good indeed. Nor are the tools and materials required overly expensive. Furthermore, small pieces can be finished in an apartment, although a large basement or garage work area is certainly more desirable and convenient.

The one overriding requirement is care. Each step should be as perfect as possible. Any rough areas, blotches, or careless slips will be magnified by the final finish coats. The most serious mistake a finisher can make is to say to himself: "That will even out later" or "I'll fix that at the next stage." It will not work. And one item that requires particular care is cleanliness, which is essential in wood finishing. Dust is a determined enemy that can ruin hours of hard work if it settles on a piece covered with wet finish. Dirt in brushes can also spell disaster by leaving cloudy smudged areas on an otherwise transparent finish.

The Steps Involved

The work of wood finishing divides into a group of separate steps or operations, none of which are particularly difficult but most of which require time. The high cost of professionally applied finishes is due only partly to the skill of the finisher. Professional finishing is costly because it requires a lot of time and patience. The work cannot be pushed—it takes 24 hours for glue to dry, 12 hours for finish to harden. Some of the more difficult finishes, such as shellac piano finishes applied by a technique known as French polishing, can literally take months. The amateur or hobbyist who can put in a few hours here and there until the job is done has a distinct advantage over the professional who must make a profit for his time.

The basic steps are repairing and removing old finish (if the task is refinishing), sanding, staining, filling, sealing, applying finish coats, and rubbing and polishing to the desired gloss and luster. Each job will not require all the steps, and some, like staining, can be omitted according to the preference of the finisher. Most finishers work from what they call a "finishing schedule." Such schedules are a step-by-step outline of the finishing process and specify the colors of stains, fillers, and final finishing materials. They are a good guide for the beginner to refer to in order to keep the necessary operations in the proper order. A sample finishing schedule that includes the maximum possible steps in a refinishing project follows. The chapters in this book follow a similar order.

FINISHING SCHEDULE

1. Remove all hardware, hinges, pulls, knobs, escutcheons, and casters from the piece. Take it apart as far as possible, removing all doors, drawers, and shelves.

2. Make any necessary repairs. Reglue loose parts, rebuild drawers, replace or correct any warped boards.

3. Remove any old finish.

4. Wash any paint remover out of the wood with trisodium phosphate, which is known as TSP in the paint trade.

5 (Optional). Bleach the wood to remove old wood stain if necessary. Also use bleach to remove any stains that have resulted from exposure to water. Remove grease stains. Chemically age the wood if desired.

6. Sand all rough spots. With sandpaper round off any sharp edges slightly to minimize the danger of chipping. Rounding off edges also prolongs the appearance of the piece—the first place finish will wear off is sharp corners and edges. Use as many grades of sandpaper as necessary but end with a fine paper. Dust and vacuum to remove all dust from sanding.

7 (Optional). Stain the wood with the desired color of stain. Allow it to dry at least overnight.

8. Seal the wood with a wash coat of either shellac or commercial sealer. Allow it to dry for at least four hours.

9 (Optional). Treat with wood toner if desired.

10 (Optional). If the piece is an open-grained wood such as oak or mahogany, fill the pores with a wood filler. The filler should be mixed with stain of a slightly darker shade than the surrounding wood. Otherwise the final finish will appear cloudy. Allow the filler to dry at least 24 hours.

11. Fill any deep scratches or dents with shellac or lacquer stick matched to the shade of the stained wood.

12 (Optional). Apply a wash coat of sealer over the filler if filler was used.

13. Sand the sealed piece with fine and very fine grades of sandpaper. Dust and vacuum carefully.

14. Apply the first coat of finishing material, thinned as necessary. Allow it to dry the designated time for that material.

15. Sand with very fine sandpaper. Dust and vacuum.

16. Apply at least one additional coat of finish, more if desired or dictated by either the finish material or application method. Allow it to dry. Sand with very fine paper and dust.

17. Apply final coat of finish. Allow it to dry for at least 48 hours.

18. Sand with the finest grade of paper possible.

19. Use pumice and oil, rottenstone, or another rubbing material to produce the desired finish: dull, satin, gloss, or highly polished.

Selecting the Finish

The earliest clear finishes were simply beeswax or oil rubbed into the wood, coat after coat. Sometimes these finishes were applied over water-based stains made from plant and mineral pigments. Their origin is lost but they probably came about as an attempt to imitate the smooth satin surface produced by wear and grease from the user's hands. Such finishes remain the most durable of all. They are built up over a long time by periodic applications of new oil or wax, each new coat removing dirt from the surface and renewing the luster of the finish.

Shellac came into wide use as a furniture finish in the eighteenth century. As finish it offered the convenience of not requiring the periodic maintenance of the oil and wax finishes. It was, however, expensive, and home-built furniture continued to get the oil-and-wax treatment or was painted. Also, much early American furniture was painted with so-called "milk paints," which were made from sour milk mixed with such pigments as animal blood. Varnish—an improvement on shellac in terms of durability—did not become widely used until the latter half of the nineteenth century. And although lacquer has been known in the West since the time of Marco Polo, it did not become a major furniture finish until synthetic types were introduced in the 1940s. Lacquer is now the dominant finish used commercially, because it sprays on easily and dries fast.

Since the development of synthetic lacquer, a wide range of finishes based on man-made resins have entered the marketplace. Many commercial varnishes are now based on polyurethanes. These are so new that we are not yet sure they are as long-lasting as shellac and varnish, but they appear to be some of the toughest finishes yet. Furthermore, they are still being improved.

There is no ideal finishing material. Each has some advantages and some disadvantages. And that is probably why most people settle on one type of finishing material and use it over and over again. They have made a compromise that they are comfortable with. Nonetheless, the choice of a finish depends on the desired appearance and a balance of the properties offered by each. The following broad classes of finishes are available:

Shellac. One of the most time-tested finishing materials. It is compatible with almost all other finishes and is widely used as a sealer before applying the final finish. Its main drawback is its poor water resistance. Water makes it turn white and cloudy. As a result, shellac is not suitable for tabletops and other surfaces exposed to water. It is, however, one of the most easily restored and maintained finishes. When it ages and dries out, it will develop cracks on the surface but these can be corrected by resoftening the shellac with alcohol.

Varnish. Like shellac, it develops cracks when it ages. But a varnish finish will last at least twenty years if it is properly applied. Varnish resists water and forms a very strong, elastic film on the wood. It requires very little maintenance and is a good finish for tables and bar tops.

Lacquer. Although it can be applied very rapidly in commercial shops and is very resistant to heat, moisture, and alcohol, lacquer is a fairly short-lived finish. Since the solvents evaporate so fast, individual coats bond poorly to each other. When the finish breaks down, it peels like the layers of an onion. It is also easy prey to solvents such as those found in nail-polish remover.

Urethane Finishes. These are extremely tough, durable materials that are resistant to most chemicals—including paint remover. In fact, they can be very difficult to remove. When they were first introduced, there were many inferior products on the market, including some that seemed to begin peeling before they were dry. Today they are much better, but it is best to stick with the products of the major manufacturers.

Penetrating Sealers. These are synthetic finishes that penetrate deeply into the wood, effectively sealing the pores and hardening the surface. They do not leave a glossy surface but are totally flat, leaving the appearance of unfinished wood. They are water washable and resist most kinds of damage to which finishes are exposed. Since they are flat, damage to the wood does not show up as it would on a highly polished surface. They may be recoated at any time.

Commercial Oil and Wax Finishes. Such products are variations on penetrating sealers. The oil finishes were popular when the "Scandinavian look" was fashionable in modern furniture. These combine a penetrating sealer with an oil that drys to a hard film. These, too, produce a flat finish. The wax products are mixtures of stains with solvents and wax. The idea is that the solvent will carry the wax and stain into the wood fibers. Some wax remains on the surface. Both are simple finishes suitable for quick finishing jobs and use on paneling. They are intended for amateur use and are not in the same class as shellac and the varnishes for applying fine furniture finishes.

Whatever type of finish is used, always buy the best-quality product available. A great deal of time and effort goes into a finishing job. Having that effort destroyed by an inferior product is pure foolishness. In addition, stick to the products of one manufacturer, particularly with thinners for synthetic varnishes and lacquers. The thinner formulated by one manufacturer for use with its products may not be compatible with the finish of another.

Tools and Supplies

Wood finishing does not require an elaborate assortment of tools or a well-equipped home workshop. Furniture that requires repair before refinishing should be selected according to the ability of the worker. For the most part, the repairs covered in this book can be made by anyone familiar with hand tools. Aside from the removers, stains, and finishes, few additional tools and supplies are needed. Essential supplies include a putty knife or scraper for removing the old finish, an assortment of various grades of abrasive paper, steel wool, and brushes. Those things—plus a nearly endless supply of newspapers, clean rags for wiping, and tin cans to hold small quantities of finish remover, stain, and solvents—are adequate for the highest quality job.

The only tool that is absolutely critical is the brush or spray equipment used to apply the finish. The final finish will only be as good as the brush or spray equipment that is used to apply it. No matter how skilled a painter may be, poor-quality equipment will result in a finish marred by runs, sags, and brush marks.

ABOUT BRUSHES

In wood finishing the most expensive brush may very well turn out to be the cheapest in the long run. There is absolutely no way that a fine finish can be applied with the types of brushes sold in shopping-center hardware departments or general hardware stores. And the salesmen in those stores are likely to have about as much knowledge of good brushes as the newsboy. Locate the best-equipped paint store in your area and ask to see the best brushes. You might also ask a professional painter where he buys his brushes.

Select a brush that feels thick and full when it is squeezed in the hand. That means that the manufacturer has not skimped on the bristles. The more bristles that a brush has, the better it holds finish and the more evenly it releases it to the work surface. The brush should also taper noticeably from the base of the bristles to their tip. In good brushes, some bristles are shorter than others—this can be observed by bending the brush and sliding it out of the hand; the short bristles will pop up when they are released. A good tapered brush will bend evenly when it is drawn across a surface in a painting motion. Test the brush on a dry surface by stopping in midstroke. The brush should be flexible enough to bend in an even curve with almost no spreading at the tip. A poor brush will spread so that the fibers separate where they contact the work surface. Such a brush will leave brush marks.

Buying a top-quality brush will probably come as a surprise to those who have been accustomed to purchasing an inexpensive brush, using it once, and throwing it away. They are expensive! A good 3-inch brush can cost as much as a gallon of finish. But like any good tool, it is not intended for a single use. With proper care a good brush can be used weekly for ten years—long after its inexpensive cousins have turned into unruly masses of frayed bristles. Each brush, however, should only be used for one finish. If a brush is used for varnish, never use it for shellac or vice versa. And once a brush has been used for stain, *never ever* use it for anything else. Staining, in fact, is the one place where corners can be cut with brushes. Since the stain is wiped into the wood, old or inexpensive brushes are perfectly adequate.

Before using a new brush remove any loose bristles by running your fingers through the brush and by spinning it between the palms of both hands and then tapping the bristles against the palm of the hand. Even the best brushes are likely to have a few loose hairs, and if they are not removed they will end up in the finish. Brushes that will be used for enamels or varnish should be conditioned by soaking them up to the top of the bristles in boiled linseed oil for two to three days. When the brush is to be used, drain out as much of the oil as possible and work out the remainder by painting it onto old newspaper.

When coats of finishing material are being applied in rapid succession it is not necessary to clean the brush each time it is used. But never lay the brush down between coats. Rather, leave it suspended in the finishing material—it can be tied to the can with twine or a hook improvised from a coat hanger—and cover both the can and the brush tightly with a plastic bag to prevent evaporation and keep out dust. For overnight storage of brushes, clean as much finishing material out of the brush as possible by painting it onto newspaper, rinse it in the appropriate solvent for the finishing material. Then wrap the brush in newspaper or brown paper and let it rest in a can that contains enough solvent to come about a third of the way up the bristles.

For long-term storage, clean varnish and enamel brushes in mineral spirits and then wash in a commercial brush cleaner (sold in paint stores). Wash out the cleaner in a solution of pure soap (such as Ivory) and water, rinse in clear water. Lay the brush on a sloping surface, with the tip downward, for a few days to dry and then wrap it in clean newspaper. Shellac brushes should be washed in household ammonia and warm water before the shellac has had time to harden, then rinsed in clear water and left to dry. If shellac has hardened in the brush, soak it overnight in alcohol and then clean with ammonia and warm water.

ABOUT SPRAY EQUIPMENT

An amateur intending to do a great deal of wood finishing or a semiprofessional such as an antique dealer may want spray equipment for applying the final finish. The expense of buying it, however, is not justified unless considerable work is contemplated. Spray application is particularly suited to enamels and to lacquers, many of which dry too rapidly to be applied by brush. With practice it is possible to apply a smooth, even coating that is far superior to that possible with a brush. In addition, coats are more even than those applied by brush and dry faster.

Conventional spray systems use a compressor to supply compressed air to a nozzle. Suction draws the finish from a cup attached to the nozzle into the nozzle where it is atomized. The minimum output of a compressor for wood finishing is 4 cubic feet a minute at a pressure of 25 pounds per square inch. This is known as a suction-feed system. Other systems, including pressure feed and hot lacquer, are suitable only for high-volume production work. The suction-feed system is adequate for most shops with a low to moderate volume of work.

Spray equipment requires the same diligent care as brushes. All finishing material must be strained to remove any dirt or lumps before going into the spray container. The spray gun should be completely disassembled and cleaned after every use.

Skillful handling of a spray gun requires practice—which can be acquired on any old piece of wood using a colored enamel that will show up missed spots. Proper thinning of material to be sprayed depends on the person spraying, the operating pressure, and the material being applied. Spray patterns, nozzle adjustment, proper distance of the gun from the work surface all come from experience as well. The objective of proper spraying is to apply an even, wet coat of material to the surface. Getting the coat wet enough so that the finish flows together evenly but does not run is the most difficult aspect of spraying.

FINDING FINISHING SUPPLIES

While most metropolitan areas have suppliers of finishing supplies, in many parts of the country sources of supplies are difficult to locate. Such items as wood fillers (not the pre-mixed Plastic Wood type), lacquer sticks, dry colors for stains, and wood veneers can be hard to find.

The best starting point is to seek out the biggest supplier of paints in your area. If that fails, try the local cabinetmakers and antique dealers that specialize in refinished furniture. But look at their finishes first—some antique dealers have no conception of a good finish. Nor do their customers. Still, many dealers may have sources of supply in the area and most will be willing to tell you where they are.

The last resort is mail order. A number of companies advertise in the nationally distributed handyman's magazines. It is a good idea, however, to stick with the largest, most reputable firms. Refer to the appendix section for the names and addresses of some additional sources of supplies.

A Place to Work

Professional woodworking shops have a room for finishing that is separated from areas where wood is sawn and sanded. Such a room isn't necessary for a smaller shop, but the principle is the same: areas where finishes are applied must be *clean*. This is especially critical when slow-drying finishes like varnish are being applied. Few things are more depressing to a finisher than coming back to a recently coated piece to find it decorated with dust that has stuck fast in the finish.

Wherever finishing is done, the environment should be made as dust-free as possible before any finish is applied. All sanding dust should be vacuumed both from the piece and from the entire room as well. The piece itself, once vacuumed, should be wiped with a tack rag to remove all traces of dust from the surface. You can buy tack rags, but it is really a waste of money. Simply dampen a clean lint-free rag in water and wring it out. Then wet it with a mixture of 1 part varnish and 1 part turpentine, wring it out until it is almost dry and store it in a sealed jar. The rag will remove minute traces of dust that have not been picked up by vacuuming.

If possible the finishing room should also be damp-mopped to keep dust down during finishing. Clean newspapers should be spread over the floor. And finally, it is not a waste of time to wear a cap or hairnet while applying finishes. That may prevent the disconcerting experience of finding that the hairs in the finish are not from the brush, but from your head.

After applying the finish, close the door to the finishing area and leave it closed until the finish has dried enough so dust will no longer stick to it. When the finish has dried enough, allow free ventilation in the room until the finish is thoroughly dry.

A Word About Safety

Wood finishing is certainly a lot less dangerous than mountain climbing. But it, like anything else, is not without its hazards. Finishers use a variety of flammable, toxic, and caustic chemicals. Accidents can and do happen.

The most obvious hazard in wood finishing is fire. Everything from paint remover to final finish and rubbing oil is flammable. A workroom is likely to contain cans of all manner of combustible materials, including alcohol, paint thinner, linseed oil, and various finishes. But a few simple precautions can avert a potential disaster:

- Always work in an area with adequate ventilation. Use finish removers outdoors wherever possible.

- Never work near an open flame or electrical motor. Do not smoke while applying finishes. Turn off electrical appliances that could make a spark; stay clear of open flames like pilot lights in furnaces and water heaters.

- Throw all oily rags and newspapers away at once. And that means outside, in a tightly closed garbage can located away from the house. Spread rags and papers out to dry if they must be left inside—spontaneous combustion will take place only when oil-soaked material is wadded together.

- Seal all cans of volatile materials tightly. Store them in an area with good ventilation, never in a closed cupboard that will allow fumes to build up to combustible or explosive levels.

- Keep a fire extinguisher nearby.

Some of the materials involved in finishing are also caustic or are strong irritants. Lye, which is sometimes used to remove paint, is highly caustic. Commercial paint removers are irritants that can cause severe injury if they get into the eyes. The best precaution is to work near a source of water. Many professional shops have emergency showers, but a faucet or a hose will suffice. And if those are not available, keep a bucket of water nearby. Flush any such materials away from the skin immediately. If it has soaked through the clothing, flush the area with water first, then get out of the clothes.

It is also a good idea to keep an eye cup handy. Aside from the danger of chemicals, particles of finish or wood can quite easily get into the eyes during sanding or dusting. You may also want to wear goggles or a respirator to protect yourself from injury.

In addition, keep a good first-aid kit so handy that you practically fall over it. A first-aid kit should contain iodine, peroxide, cotton swabs, scissors, tweezers, burn ointment, bicarbonate of soda, bandages, gauze pads, and adhesive tape. And if you are using power tools, it is far from frivolous to keep a tourniquet around. Almost every experienced worker, even the most careful and skilled, has had some kind of accident in his life. It is sheer vanity to think that it will never happen to you. And quick action and the right materials within reach can make an important difference.

2

Repairs Before Refinishing

The time, effort, and care required to apply a good, new finish to a piece of furniture is wasted unless the furniture is sound and in good condition. The first step in any refinishing job should be a thorough examination of the piece to identify those places where repairs are required and to judge the potential value of the piece against the time required to make necessary repairs. A badly damaged piece that was inferior to start with may not be worth the effort of repairing and refinishing.

The person buying old furniture with an eye toward refinishing it should be familiar with the signs of good craftsmanship, capable of recognizing the common furniture woods, and able to determine the extent of repairs required. At the very least, the level of craftsmanship, quality of the wood, and the amount of repair called for should be reflected very strongly in the price. That ancient adage, *caveat emptor,* can prove to be painfully true to the untutored individual who finds himself for the first time in a barn filled with old furniture that is covered with grime, cobwebs, and layers of paint, no price tags in sight and the whole establishment presided over by some old duffer who looks at the make of car parked outside before he quotes a price.

With valuable antiques, attempting to remove all signs of

wear and damage can significantly decrease their value. In fact, on some the old finish, if it is original, is better left alone. Certain finishes, such as decorative paint or stencils, are sometimes a major part of the value of an antique. And, depending on the value of the piece and the complexity of the repair required, in some cases it may make sense to take the piece to a skilled restorer. But for most furniture, minor repairs such as regluing loose joints, filling cracks and dents, removing warps, and patching veneer, can be accomplished by the moderately skilled amateur.

Recognizing Quality

Aside from style and design, the value of furniture rests in the workmanship and the quality of materials that went into its manufacture. Whatever the style and however good the design, if the piece is a cheap knockoff, poorly constructed from inferior wood, it is scarcely worth the work required to repair and finish it.

Learning to identify the basic marks of quality is relatively simple. While techniques have changed and methods of construction can be used as an indication of age, they have nothing to do with craftsmanship. There has always been well-built furniture and poorly made furniture. In most cases, the better woods were used for the better furniture. Some finely constructed furniture is made from pine and other softwoods, but generally, pieces made from softwoods tend to be more utilitarian and were not executed with the care of furniture made from hardwood.

This, of course, is not to say that inferior furniture has never been made from the fine hardwoods, including cherry, walnut, mahogany, fruitwood, or teak, but it does hold true that hardwoods require more skill to work and produce a more valuable finished product. As a result, the finer woods were used by the better craftsmen. An exception is the mass-produced oak furniture made during the early part of this century. But even here, most of the utilitarian oak furniture was built for heavy use and is very durable although simply designed and constructed.

The best way to spot craftsmanship in furniture is to examine a drawer, door, or an edge. A drawer can tell a great deal about the quality of a piece. First, do the drawers operate smoothly? If not, wear and warping may be responsible but, more likely than not, the glides were not carefully designed and constructed. A third glide in the center, put there to assure even operation, is a good indication of quality. Also, are there dust shields under the drawers? Dust shields form a bottom to the area occupied by the drawer. They show that the furniture maker was concerned about the function of the drawer—to keep things clean in storage—and chose not to cut corners where they would not show.

The construction of the drawer itself will also betray telltale signs of quality workmanship. The most solid way to join the body of the drawer to the front is a dovetail joint. The least secure but easiest way is simply to butt the sides of the

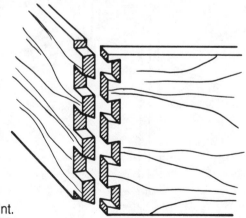

Dovetail joint.

drawer against the edges of the front and secure it with glue and nails. Dovetails joining the back of the drawer to the sides are a further mark of quality.

The same applies to doors. Raised panels are an indication of quality. Joints mitred at a 45-degree angle in the frame of a paneled door are not. Also note the care with which the door is mounted in its frame. On high-quality furniture, doors will be equipped with stops that prevent infiltration of dust.

Another indication of good craftsmanship is the use of glue blocks. These are usually small triangular blocks of wood that are placed in inside corners to brace the piece against lateral motion. In case-goods (that is, furniture such as chests and dressers), they should be located along the

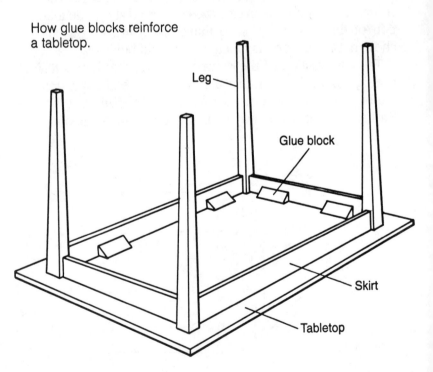

How glue blocks reinforce a tabletop.

Leg

Glue block

Skirt

Tabletop

corners where the sides and back join the top and along the joint formed by the sides and the back. On tables they are placed along the edge of the top where it joins the skirt and are sometimes used to brace the legs against the skirt. Although screws are frequently used to attach tops to tables, glue blocks provide an additional margin of stability. The absence of glue blocks is usually a sign of poor workmanship. And the more glue blocks that are used, the better the piece should be. Each side of a piece should have at least three glue blocks. In the better furniture they are placed about 4 inches apart.

Contrary to popular belief, the use of veneer in furniture is not a sign of inexpensive and poor construction. Before the machine age, cutting wood into thin slices to make veneers and matching and applying that veneer was a highly skilled process. Veneer gave the craftsman an additional means of decoration. Veneers cut from a single board could be matched and reversed so that the figure of a particularly beautiful piece of wood could be repeated in a process called book-matching. The extremely beautiful grain patterns in burl and crotch wood can be used only in the form of veneer, because the wood itself is too weak to be used structurally.

Today, most furniture is made from cabinet-grade, or lumber-core, plywood. This is really nothing more than a series of boards glued together edge-to-edge under high pressure. The boards themselves have usually been force-dried and treated to resist warping. The wooden core is then covered with sheets of select veneer. The result is a building material that is much more resistant to warping and humidity changes than older furniture glued under much lower pressure in the craftsman's shop. Drawers and doors of furniture built with this material have much less tendency to stick in damp weather and are much less likely to come unglued during the dry winter months.

What gave veneer its bad name was its wide use in low-cost, mass-produced furniture early in this century. These pieces, however, are easy to spot. For one thing, they tend to be extremely light in weight, with panels that are little thicker than the veneer itself. If the piece is of poor quality, it is the fault of much more than the veneer. It will be thin and light, and will lack any of the other signs of good workmanship.

When buying old furniture, it's a good idea to carry a small penknife or a razor blade. Most dealers in used furniture will let you carefully scrape the old finish from a small spot to examine the wood. First, identify the wood and then look to see if the piece is solid or veneered. Scraping a back edge may expose the edge of the veneer. In addition, the grain, and even the kind of wood, will not match on opposite sides of veneered boards. On older furniture the veneers were cut by hand and are much thicker than those used now—up to $1/8$ inch thick. Present veneers range from $1/32$ to $1/64$ inch thick. As a result, modern veneer is delicate—it cannot withstand years of hard wear nor can it be heavily sanded without cutting all the way through.

Designs made from different veneers or simply decorative panels of fine veneers such as burl were frequently used on drawer fronts and door panels. If you are looking at a heavily painted piece that is made from good hardwood, scrape a likely spot to see if fine, highly figured veneers were used. A seam in the front of a drawer or in the center of the top indicates that book-matched panels of veneer may have been used, with the grain repeating in mirror-image on each side of the division.

These few marks of good craftsmanship are only a starting point, but they can protect against the purchase of inferior furniture. Still, anyone interested enough in furniture to want to refinish or restore it would do well to obtain one of the many books available on furniture making. Methods of construction, including everything from glue blocks to veneer thickness, dovetails and joints, and the use of screws and nails, can tell a great deal. They are signs of the age of a piece and where it was made, and can sometimes be used to identify individual furniture makers.

Inspecting for Damage

Before you begin to refinish an old piece of furniture, it should be put into sound condition. At a minimum, all loose joints should be tightened, major cracks filled, blisters and blemishes in veneer repaired, and warps removed. More extensive repairs—such as replacing missing drawers, doors, panels, or other pieces—can be attempted if the value of the piece warrants the effort and expense. These repairs are beyond the scope of this book and in most cases require the talents of a skilled woodworker. The expense of rebuilding severely damaged furniture can be justified with valuable antiques.

In most cases, the repairs required on old furniture are relatively easy for the moderately skilled amateur to accomplish. They are mainly the result of wear and age. Even the best old glues weaken with age, wood shrinks, and carelessness and accidents take their toll. Wooden furniture is dynamic; it reacts to its environment. In the dry months of the winter, the wood shrinks away from the glue at joints. And the glue dries out; it loses its elasticity, grows brittle, and pulls away from the wood. The result is loose, wobbly furniture. And in the summer, humidity causes the wood to swell, some finishes become sticky, veneer may blister, and large flat areas warp.

Before any refinishing operations are contemplated, carefully inspect the furniture to be refinished. On a level surface, wobble the piece to be sure that it sits solidly on the floor. If not, a leg may have worn down. That will mean repairing it or shortening the others to make them all uniform. Also, push against the frame of the piece to identify loose joints that will have to be reglued. Examine all surfaces for dents, gouges, blemishes, and blisters in the veneer. Check for warps that may be serious enough to need correcting. Check doors and drawers for loose or damaged panels or parts.

When you start working on a piece, remove all hardware and take the piece apart as much as possible. This will prevent damage during repair and refinishing, make it easier to remove the old finish, and make the piece lighter and easier to handle. Whenever possible, complete all repairs before removing the old finish—the finish will protect the wood from damage while you work and prevent glue from getting on bare wood, where it will seal the wood and prevent any stain from being absorbed.

About Glue

The majority of the needed repairs on most old pieces of furniture will involve glue. Glue is the principal means of holding furniture together. Even where screws are used, glue is always applied to the joint before the screws to provide additional strength. In fact in many cases it is the glue that provides the strength; the screws serve more to clamp the joint while the glue dries. Nails are rarely used in furniture making because they lack the holding power of either screws or glue. They usually represent poor workmanship or inept repairs. Nails should be avoided in repairs, except in a few special cases. Dowels, however, are frequently used to align and strengthen furniture joints.

TYPES OF GLUE

The success of a repair job depends on the selection of the proper glue for the job. A number of glues are available, and each type has properties that recommend it for certain types of repairs (see table on p. 29). This is not to say that each repair job will require a different and specialized type of glue. Glues fall into several broad categories and most furniture repairers develop preferences and use one type for most work.

The main groups of glues useful in furniture repair are:

Liquid Animal and Fish Glues. For several hundred years at least, these were the only glues used in making furniture. They are made by boiling animal hides, horns, and hooves, or fish scales, until they form a gelatinous mass; this is allowed to harden and then broken into flakes. Animal glues are available in liquid form in a wide variety of containers and sizes. Formerly they were sold in dry sheets which were mixed in the shop and held in heated glue pots. They are viscous amber liquids that have a faintly fetid odor. They form a strong bond and can be used in most general woodworking. Their main drawbacks are that they are water-soluble and can stain some light-colored woods. In addition, they do not resist high temperatures and dryness very well. Nonetheless, the amount of old furniture that is still strong and firm after many years of use testifies to their effectiveness, and they are still preferred by many craftspeople.

White Glue. This is a newer type of glue based on vinyl resins. It comes in liquid form in small applicator bottles and in larger containers of a gallon and more. It forms strong joints, doesn't stain wood, and can be used equally well to bond wood, paper, leather, cardboard, and fabrics. Because of its ease of application it has become one of the most widely used general-purpose glues. Like animal glues, it is affected by heat and moisture.

Casein Glues. These are glues that are made from casein,

an albuminlike component of milk. They are sold in powdered form and must be mixed with water before they can be used. Casein glues will stain some woods, but they are the best glues available for bonding oily woods such as teak. Teak has so much natural oil in the wood that it is difficult to glue—the property that makes it so widely used in boatbuilding is a disadvantage in furniture. The glue sets fast, but requires high clamping pressures, and will form strong joints. It is not, however, waterproof, but it will bond ill-fitting joints. This is the only woodworking glue that can be used at low temperatures.

Resorcinol-Resin Glues. This is the best type of glue for wood that will be used outdoors. It is completely waterproof and forms a strong bond that resists heat and cold. It is not attacked by fungus or mildew, which sometimes affect outdoor furniture during damp weather. Resorcinol glues consist of two components—a pale brown powder and a thick amber liquid. The components are mixed into a paste just before use. The resulting glue must be used at temperatures above 70° F. At lower temperatures it will set but the joints will be weaker. These glues have the disadvantages of leaving dark stains on wood surfaces. Also, they shrink significantly when they set, so that they do not work very well on loose joints.

Plastic-Resin Glues. Also known as synthetic-resin glues, these strong adhesives are sold in powder form and mixed with water. With smooth and close-fitting joints, plastic-resin glues form joints that are stronger than the wood itself and are waterproof as well. Nor do they stain easily discolored hardwoods like mahogany or oak and, like resorcinol glues, they are completely resistant to mold and rot. Parts bonded with plastic-resin glue must be kept tightly clamped for at least 10 hours at temperatures of 70° F or above for joints to reach maximum strength.

Contact Cement. Contact cements have limited use in furniture repair but they are useful in applying plastic laminates,

GLUES

Types	Uses	Advantages	Disadvantages
Liquid animal and fish glues	Cabinet and woodwork	Easy to apply, strong	Steady dry heat or water may weaken
White glue	Wood, cloth, cork, paper	Makes strong joints; doesn't stain wood; sets fast	Steady dry heat or water may weaken
Casein glues	Cabinet and indoor woodwork	Will bond ill-fitting joints; strong, sets fast. Use for oily woods (e.g., teak)	May stain light woods; mixing required
Resorcinol-resin glues	Exterior work	Waterproof, strong, and durable; resists heat, cold, and fungus	Leaves dark stains on wood; may be painted; mixing required
Plastic-resin glues	Indoor woodwork	Strong; does not stain wood; resists heat, water, and fungus	Mixing required
Contact cement	Laminates, wallboard, wood, cloth, leather, rubber	Instant bonding without clamps; resists water, heat, fungus	Not strong enough for parts under stress; very flammable; fumes are harmful

such as Formica, and in gluing the occasional leather or cloth top that a refinisher may encounter. Contact cements bond instantly and require no clamping. They cannot, however, be used on finished surfaces—they contain solvents that affect finishes as strongly as paint remover. The adhesive is applied to both surfaces to be bonded. It is allowed to set for 20 to 30 minutes. When it is dry enough that a piece of brown paper laid on its surface does not stick, it is ready for bonding. Align the two surfaces but keep them separated by a sheet of brown paper. Then slide out the paper and work over the surface, starting from one corner, with a roller designed for the purpose or a rolling pin. The parts will bond tightly immediately.

Applying Glue

Selecting the proper glue is only part of the job. No matter how good the glue is, joints will not hold if the glue is improperly applied. All surfaces to be glued must be absolutely clean and fit together tightly.

When regluing an old joint that has become loose, the first—and most important—step is to remove all the old glue from the joint. Wood can be glued to wood with the result that the bond will be stronger than the wood itself, but if you try to bond old glue to old glue, you won't end up with a strong joint. If a glue joint has come apart, the old glue is usually so dry and brittle that it can easily be scraped off with a small sharp knife or a razor blade. After the excess has been removed, the part should be sanded to assure that all the glue has been removed. Use coarse sandpaper, however; the new glue will hold better if the mating surfaces are slightly rough. Cavities, such as the holes for chair rungs, are difficult to clean out. They too, can be scraped out with a small knife but, in the case of round holes, a standard drill bit can also be used. Find the size that precisely fits the hole—most chair rungs are ³/₈ inch—and work the bit into the hole, using a tap handle or holding it securely with a pair of pliers. But be careful not to enlarge the hole or a loose joint will result.

The old wood glues, such as those made from hide or fish, as well as modern white glue can be softened for removal with hot vinegar. Wipe on heated vinegar and keep the part moist, then rub it off with steel wool. In most cases, however, scraping is easier.

Glue must be applied evenly to all bonding surfaces for a good joint to result. The best way to apply glue is with a fairly stiff brush small enough to cover the areas being glued adequately. The glue should literally be "scrubbed" into the wood so that each piece is evenly coated and well-wetted by the glue. When gluing oily wood, such as teak, it is a good idea to wash the surfaces with alcohol or lacquer thinner before applying the glue—this will remove some of the surface oil that would otherwise weaken the joint.

After coating all surfaces evenly with glue, press or tap the parts together until they have mated snugly. Wash off all the excess glue that oozes out of the joint and clamp the work tightly. In fact, if no glue oozes, you have not used enough.

Clamping Glued Joints

Virtually all glue joints require pressure to develop the maximum strength. The one exception is glue blocks—the small blocks of wood used to reinforce corner joints. These small triangular blocks are coated with glue and slid into place with hand pressure. Apply glue both to the two sides of the glue block and to the corner surfaces to which it will be attached. Snug the block into the corner and push it forward until you feel the glue grab. By sliding the glue block through the glue, you work any air bubbles out, and force excess glue out of the joint.

All other glue joints, however, require clamping. A variety of excellent clamps have been designed for this purpose but, if they are used only rarely, it is possible to improvise or get by with one or two clamps. Nonetheless, the best joints will be those that are properly clamped and allowed to set under considerable, but even, pressure.

The commercial woodworker or the skilled amateur who does a good deal of furniture work will need to have the appropriate clamps on hand. The common C-clamp, found in many home workshops, is never appropriate, however. These clamps are intended for metalworking. Their small faces can deeply gouge wood and their screw mechanisms are not designed to apply enough pressure for wood gluing. They are never found in woodworking shops. The main types of clamps found in most woodworking shops are:

Bar Clamps. These clamps are essential for gluing large pieces of furniture such as tabletops and case goods. They consist of a metal bar anywhere from 24 to 72 inches long, an adjustable face, and a screw clamp. The adjustable face slides along the bar and can be locked into place to fit any length of workpiece. The clamp is tightened by a screw mechanism attached to one end. These are extremely accurate clamps but care must be taken when using them: it's easy to apply too much pressure and they are strong enough literally to crush the wood.

A variation of the bar clamp, which is designed specifically for furniture manufacturing and repair, has three separate faces—a flat one, a flat one that swivels, and a concave one. It is extremely versatile and can be used to clamp angular pieces; the curved faces make it ideal for gluing chairs.

Pipe Clamps. These are an inexpensive alternative to bar clamps. They consist of a sliding face with a clutch mechanism to lock it into place that is designed to fit over a length

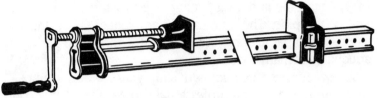

Bar clamp

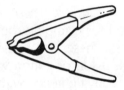

Spring clamp

Handscrew clamp

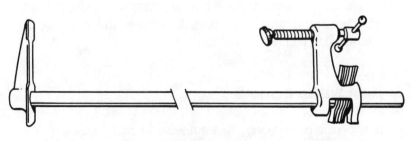

Pipe clamp

of ³/₄ -inch pipe and a tightening face that threads over one end of the pipe. The pipe can be any length. They are not as precise as bar clamps, but they cost less and are perfectly adequate for many jobs.

Hand Screws. Also known simply as "wood clamps," these are the mark of a professional cabinet shop. They consist of two wooden jaws that are adjusted by two threaded rods that connect them. That arrangement permits the jaws to be offset or the clamp to be closed tightly on surfaces that are not parallel. Since the jaws are wood and they have a large surface area, they can be used in direct contact with the wood being glued. They are available with maximum openings from 3 to 10 inches.

Web Clamps. These are specialized clamps that are intended for clamping round or irregular shapes, such as the pedestal bases for some round tables. They consist of a tough nylon or cotton web that is pulled up tight by hand and finally tightened with a crank-type screw or a wrench.

Others. There are also a number of highly specialized clamp designs that are quite expensive; unless they are used regularly, their purchase cannot be justified. Edge-gluing clamps, for example, are used to hold thin pieces of veneer along edges of tabletops. And corner clamps are designed for clamping corners of frames where two pieces of wood are glued at right angles to each other. Also, spring clamps, rather like large clothespins, are used where light pressure is required and no stress is placed on the parts being glued. Such cases include reattaching applied carvings and molding or gluing small patches or veneer.

IMPROVISED CLAMPS

It is possible, however, to improvise in many cases. While web clamps are ideal for gluing chairs, rope tourniquets work almost as well. They can be used to apply even clamping pressure to a variety of shapes, including dressers and chests. Simply pass a length of rope twice around the article and tie the ends together tightly. Place a short length of wood between the ropes and twist the doubled rope until it is tight enough. Then slide the end of the wooden stick behind a rung or against a face of the piece so that the tourniquet cannot unwind.

A homemade wedge clamp can also be used in place of bar or pipe clamps to glue several boards edge to edge to form a large flat surface, such as a tabletop. To make a wedge clamp, saw a board, about 4 to 6 inches wide and about 12 inches long, on a diagonal so that it forms two wedges. Butt the piece to be glued against a wall or nail another board as a stop to a flat surface. Set the two wedges,

Clamping a chair with a rope tourniquet.

offset a few inches, against the opposite side of the work-piece. Then nail the outer wedge securely in place. Apply glue to the joints, make sure the pieces are properly aligned, and then drive the inner wedge back toward its original position until glue oozes from the joints. To prevent buckling, it is a good idea to place some heavy weights (a bucket of water, bricks, or cement blocks work well) on the top surface. Be careful not to apply too much pressure, or it is almost certain to buckle.

USING CLAMPS

Extreme care must always be taken when tightening clamps. The wood must always be protected from direct contact with the clamp, especially if the clamp has metal faces or faces with small areas. Except for handscrews, which have wooden

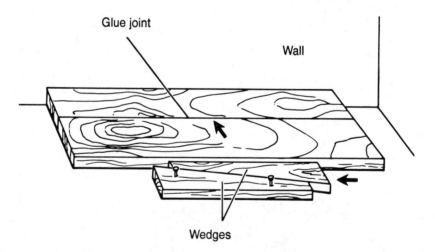

Gluing edges with an improvised wedge clamp: hammering in the wedge applies even pressure to the glue joint.

jaws, all clamps should be used with a block of scrap wood between the jaws and the article being glued.

The wooden blocks used with clamps also distribute the pressure of the clamp. This assures that all areas of the glue joint are exposed to nearly equal pressure, and it also protects the wood of the article being glued from being damaged by compression from the clamp. If clamps are tightened too much, the fibers of the wood will be compressed. Such compression damage will not show until the piece is filled or stained. The wood will accept less filler because the pores have been pressed closed. In addition, these areas will stain darker because fibers have been broken and driven closer together.

Always tighten clamps slowly and carefully. Let the glue ooze out of the joint. When the joint seems to be tightly pressed together, add only slightly more pressure. Tearing or snapping sounds coming from the wood are sure signs that the pressure is excessive and damaging the piece. Be sure to wipe away as much of the excess glue as possible. If a clamp must be placed over a seam from which glue will ooze, always cover that area with a piece of waxed paper. This will prevent the wood block, or, with hand screws, the clamp itself, from being bonded to the surface.

Most glues require clamping for at least 12 hours, and 24 hours is almost never too long to assure that the glue has thoroughly dried and reached its maximum strength. Keep the clamped piece at a temperature above 70° F, and avoid excessively high humidity.

Regluing Old Furniture

Generally, regluing should be done before beginning any refinishing operations. The exception is if you are planning to remove an old finish with lye or in a dip-stripping tank—these solutions destroy glue, so the piece is likely to need regluing after it is stripped.

GLUING CHAIRS

Probably the trickiest gluing job encountered with furniture, and the most frequent, is chairs. They are exposed to a great deal of abuse during normal use, are quite delicate, and have a large number of critical glue joints that are exposed to stress. In gluing any piece of furniture, alignment is important. If, for example, the sides of a dresser are reglued without making sure the piece is square when it is clamped, the drawers may no longer fit. The problem with chairs is similar but even worse. As they are clamped, they have a tendency to twist. The unfortunate result is that often the legs of a reglued chair do not all reach the floor.

The best way to glue a chair is to take it apart as far as possible and reglue it in sections. First glue and clamp the back and front legs with their connecting rungs and clamp them securely. When the glue is nearly dry but still pliable, add the side rungs and the seat. Before tightening the clamps, place a weight of about 100 pounds on the seat. This will insure that all four legs remain on the floor while the glue dries.

GLUING CRACKS

Another common gluing problem comes from the cracks that often appear in tabletops and other flat surfaces. If a crack is too wide, it may need to be filled, but some smaller cracks can be glued and drawn closed with clamps. This, of course, is a nearly invisible repair job. Extremely wide cracks, however, are sometimes caused by the shrinkage of the wood in a particular area. Trying to close such a crack is likely to split the wood further. Any crack more than ⅛ inch wide is better left alone or filled. Some wide cracks can be repaired by splitting the piece entirely apart, truing both edges and regluing, but the crack has to be very straight and it requires a skilled joiner to cut the edges so that they mate precisely without planing away too much wood.

The only way to determine if a crack can be glued shut is to try it. Try clamping it closed, applying pressure very gently; if it closes, you are in business. But at any sounds of distress from the wood, give up. There is always the risk that the crack will split wide open.

If a trial clamping indicates that a crack is a candidate for glue, drive a small wooden wedge gently into the crack to open it up slightly. Again, this is fraught with peril, so insert the wedge very slowly and carefully (if it sounds like it may be enlarging the crack, remove the wedge). Then use a thin knifeblade, a piece of a broken hacksaw blade, or small nail to clean as much of the accumulated dirt out of the crack as possible. After loosening the dirt, you can blow or vacuum it out of the crack. Then use a toothpick or a small brush and carefully work glue into the crack and clamp it tightly closed. Allow the glue to set for at least 24 hours.

Occasionally, wide cracks will open up on tabletops because the wood has shrunk and pulled apart the glue joints between the individual boards. In such cases the boards can be reglued, but the tabletop must first be removed, because the screws holding it to the skirt will prevent the crack from being drawn together. Remove the top, clean the dirt from the edges of the individual boards and roughen them slightly by cutting fine cross-hatches with a knife or very lightly with a hacksaw blade. Then reglue the boards, being extremely careful that they are aligned properly.

The screwholes on the underside of the tabletop will be out of alignment as the result of closing the gap in the top.

Center the top on the skirt and mark for new screw holes. Drill new holes in the skirt as well; you don't want new holes right beside the old, because they won't hold. Reinforce the joint with new glue blocks (see p. 31).

TIGHTENING LOOSE JOINTS

Sometimes the wood has shrunk with age so much that joints are too loose to hold glue well. This is a frequent problem with chair rungs. But there are several tricks that can be used to tighten loose joints. The most common is to force flat hardwood toothpicks into the joint after the glue has been applied. Some people also use sticks from wooden kitchen matches, but these are made from softwood and do not hold as well. The back of a stiff knifeblade or the edge of a chisel works very well to slide them into place. The protruding ends should be cut off flush with the joint immediately and the excess glue wiped away before the joint is clamped.

Thin strips of cloth can also be used to tighten rungs or mortise joints. Cut two narrow strips from an old pillowcase or other old piece of cloth (cotton is preferable because it will absorb glue whereas synthetics will not). The strips should be slightly narrower than the narrowest part of the joint that fits into the socket into which it will be glued. Lay the strips over the end of the part to be glued in a cross pattern, apply glue, and force into the socket. Cut the ends off flush where they protrude from the joint.

Mortise-and-tenon joints and other square-sided joints can be tightened by driving wooden wedges or shims along one or two sides of the tenon. The wedge should be coated with glue and driven into the assembled and glue-coated joint. The wedge, or shim, should be the same width as the tenon. In cases where the tenon is completely hidden by an overlapping edge, a wedge can be placed in the mortise before the joint is put together. However, precise measurement is necessary—if the wedge is too large it may be impossible to force the joint together, and too much pressure could easily split the wood.

Some furniture designs have rungs and tenons that go completely through the piece to which they are glued. When such joints become loose it is an easy matter to tighten them with a wedge. Many, in fact, were tightened with wedges when they were made, and simply inserting a thicker wedge will restore them to a tight fit. Where wedges were not used, cut a slit in the end of the rung or tenon with a thin-bladed saw, assemble the joint with glue, and drive a hardwood wedge into the slit. Wipe off the excess glue and trim the wedge flush with the surface.

Screws can also be used to tighten some joints, but they are considered the least acceptable type of repair. In joints where the pocket cut for a rung or tenon does not go all the way through the piece it is cut into, a screw can be run into the end of the rung or tenon through the wood that forms the bottom of the hole. The screw will pull the pieces together. The screw head should be countersunk so that it can be hidden by a small plug of wood or a piece of dowel. The danger in such repairs is that the wood at the end of the socket will not be thick enough to hold a screw well and that flexing during use will cause the wood to split around the screw.

Rungs that reach into sockets can also be tightened with wedges but it is tricky. Cut a slot in the end of the rung and set the tip of the wedge in place in the slot, but not all the way in. Apply glue to the rung and socket, and then drive the rung home with a rubber, rawhide, or wooden mallet. The wedge will butt against the bottom of the socket. As the rung is driven into place it will force the wedge into the slot and spread the rung. But if the wedge is too large, the piece will split; if it is too thin, it will not do any good.

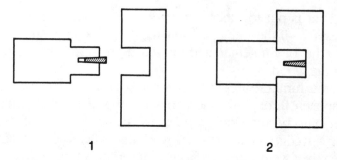

Tightening a chair rung with a wedge: (1) a small wooden wedge is fitted into a slot cut in the chair rung; (2) glue is applied to the joint and the rung is driven into place, forcing the wedge into the slot so that it expands the rung and tightens the joint.

There are also commercial products available for expanding chair joints. They consist of chemicals that cause the wood to swell. Sometimes they work and sometimes they do not. But there is no harm in trying. They are sold by some paint and hardware stores.

Dowels

Many furniture joints are strengthened with dowels. These wooden pins connect two pieces of wood across the joint and reinforce the joint while remaining invisible. They are commonly used to secure arms to chairs, to join the various boards that make up a tabletop, and in other places where pieces of wood are butted together but are exposed to lateral pressure. In many cases when furniture requires repair it will be because a doweled joint has been broken. This requires replacing the dowel or adding new ones in its place.

Special wooden pegs for doweling joints are available from some lumberyards and suppliers of woodworking supplies. They are cut from hardwood, and are 2 inches long and ⅜ inch in diameter. Spiral grooves are cut into their sides to allow the glue and air that they displace to flow freely from the hole as they are driven home. However, if specially made pegs are not available, short lengths of hardwood dowel of the type sold at lumber yards will suffice. These will work best if their ends are beveled slightly either with a knife or pencil sharpener or by rubbing against a piece of coarse sandpaper. A shallow groove cut along at least one side will free trapped air and glue. Such grooves can be easily cut with a hacksaw blade.

Holes for dowels should be snug but not so tight that the dowel cannot be pushed into place with hand pressure alone. They should also be drilled so that they are slightly longer than the dowel—¼ inch of excess at each end of a 2-inch dowel is adequate. The commercially available dowels are made for a proper fit when a ⅜-inch drill bit is used.

Drilling holes for dowels requires a certain amount of care. The holes must be absolutely perpendicular to the gluing face of the wood and they must be aligned so that the two pieces are accurately aligned. Special drilling jigs can be purchased fairly inexpensively. These are clamped to the gluing face of the wood. They position the hole and hold the drill bit perpendicular. Without such a jig, holes must be carefully marked on each face so that they are in the precise center of the board and are directly opposite each other. This can be done with careful measuring. Another way to mark holes for dowels is with an inexpensive tool called a dowel-centering pin. It fits into the hole drilled in one edge and has a sharp

Doweled joint.

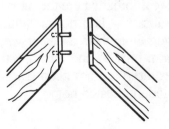

point that will mark the center of the hole to be drilled in the mating surface when the two pieces are pressed together.

When a jig is not used, the drill can be held perpendicular by drilling next to a small carpenter's square. The depth of the holes may be controlled by attaching an inexpensive depth gauge to the drill bit or by marking the bit with a small piece of tape.

Where existing dowels have broken off, drill the old dowel out of the hole and replace it with a new dowel of the appropriate diameter. To remove the old dowel, first mark the center by making a small hole with a nail, icepick, or a punch. Then drill a small guide hole and enlarge it with a bigger bit. If the dowel turns out to be harder wood than that used to build the furniture being repaired, the drill may develop the annoying habit of slipping off the dowel and cutting into the wood at its edges. In such cases, it may be easier to leave the broken dowel in place and set a new one nearby. If there is room, two small dowels can be far stronger than simply replacing a broken one, particularly if the hole must be widened excessively.

Correcting Warps

Any piece of furniture with large, flat surfaces—such as tables, chests, and dressers—is prone to warping. This is especially true if the piece has been left outdoors or stored in a damp place. And warping can result if furniture is moved from one place to another where the moisture content of the wood changes abruptly. It is not uncommon to buy a perfectly fine-looking table from a dealer who has stored it in the loft of a barn, only to find the top curling dramatically a few days after the piece has been placed in the dry environment of a modern, heated home.

Warping results when different parts of a piece of wood absorb moisture at different rates. If moisture can penetrate the underside of a board, the wood there expands. But if the top has been sealed with a finish, it will absorb moisture much more slowly. The expansion of the underside will cause the board to curl upward at the edges. The reverse will be true if the underside loses moisture rapidly—then the edges of the piece will curl downward.

Such warpage is a particular problem with old furniture in which only the surfaces that show were coated with finish. Some woodworkers argue that the custom of finishing only one side allowed the wood to "breathe" and remain in equilibrium with the moisture content of the air. A slightly less mystical view is that some early furniture makers saw little sense in wasting expensive materials and labor on finishing parts that were not visible. Whatever the reason, that practice leaves wood wide open to warping. Common practice today is to seal all surfaces of the wood with finish. While no finish is completely impervious to moisture, all surfaces will absorb or lose moisture at approximately the same rate. And while the wood may swell or contract slightly, it will do it evenly without warping.

Fortunately, many warps can be corrected. The theory is simple—bring the moisture content back into balance and the board will revert to its original shape. Then secure it tightly so that the pressure will counteract its tendency to change shape. The easiest way to accomplish this, and one that often works, is to place the board on damp grass on a sunny day. Set the board so that the bulge, or convex, face is upward. That way, the side with the highest moisture content will be dried by the sun. Meanwhile, the underside will absorb moisture from the ground. After one to three hours, the warp should have ceased to be.

When the board has flattened out, remove it to a shaded area (or inside) and allow it to dry out evenly. Set it on several level scraps of wood set perpendicular to the grain, and place several more on top of the board. Then lay another board on top of that and weight it down with bricks or other heavy objects to hold it flat as it dries; the small pieces of wood will allow air to circulate evenly. Leave it for several days.

Similar results can be obtained indoors by laying the board on damp burlap in front of the furnace or under heat lamps. Warps can also be removed by steaming the wood and then clamping or weighting it to hold it flat. You'll have to find a woodworking or boatbuilding shop that has a steam cabinet for bending wood. Still another method is to cut parallel grooves into the back of a warped board. These provide joints that permit the board to be forced into a flat position when clamped and screwed into place, but they also weaken the wood.

After the warp has been removed, all surfaces of the wood should be sealed with either varnish or clear shellac. But seal only when the wood is thoroughly dried and during a period of low humidity. Any moisture sealed into the wood will come back to haunt the refinisher. Eventually any finish that is applied will be lifted off by the escaping moisture and, once again, the board may warp.

To protect against future warping, the board should be held in place securely. Use additional screws and glue blocks to resist the tendency to warp. Further protection can be provided by reinforcing the underside of a warped board with cleats. These are simply pieces of stout hardwood that are glued and screwed across the grain on the underside of such things as tabletops. They are particularly useful in reinforcing free-hanging table leaves, which are prone to warping because they are unsupported. One or two cleats are usually sufficient for a tabletop; two or three may be required for table wings. Use strips of hardwood such as oak 2 or 3 inches wide. Space them evenly, bed them in glue, and screw them down securely with screws set about 4 inches apart in a staggered pattern to prevent splitting. Be careful that the screws are not so long that they come through the surface of the wood. Then clamp the cleats until the glue has completely set.

Seasonal swelling and warping is also a problem with drawers. The best solution to drawers that open easily in the winter but require a major fight in the summer is to seal the wood on all surfaces. This requires lying in wait for the wood. At a time when all the drawers work smoothly, take them out and give them at least two coats of a good wood sealer on all surfaces. Seal the drawer glides as well, if they are wood. Paraffin wax, the same type used for canning jars or obtained from old candles, makes an excellent lubricant for drawer glides. It can be simply rubbed on the glides or they can be painted with melted paraffin.

But the best technique—and one that will last for years—is to impregnate the wood by heating the surfaces with a medium hot iron (be careful not to use too much heat) and then to rub them with a block of wax. The paraffin will melt and penetrate the wood. Two coats provides a nearly permanent gliding surface. Some people recommend using beeswax as a lubricant. Don't! It becomes gummy with age, and the drawer will soon stick more than it did in the beginning.

Removing Dents

Wood is compressible; when it is hit with a heavy object it will dent. Minor dents can be removed by swelling the wood back to its original shape with water or steam. Deep, sharp-sided dents such as one caused by a hard hammer blow usually have to be filled or patched. In such cases the wood fibers have been crushed and broken and will not swell back to their earlier configuration.

Since the wood must absorb moisture, you'll have to remove the finish before trying to raise a dent. The best time to repair dents is after the piece has been stripped and washed. Sometimes dents can be raised on finished surfaces, but the process is very slow and the finish is almost inevitably damaged by the water and must later be restored or replaced.

The technique is simply to cover the dent with a piece of clean cloth or blotting paper and keep the area wet until the wood has swelled even with the surface. The process can be hastened by pricking small pinholes into the dent, especially if the finish is still on the piece. Faster results and success with more stubborn dents can be achieved by adding heat. Apply a steam iron at a fairly low setting directly to the damp cloth or blotting paper. This will force steam into the wood. But, whatever method is used, be prepared to spend a little time—wood can absorb moisture only so fast.

Filling Cracks and Dents

Cracks, dents, blemishes, and nail and screw holes can be filled with several materials to leave a smooth surface for the final finish. Use them only in small areas, however, because they are always visible through any finish except paint. Even though they provide a smooth surface and can be colored to match the final finish, they lack the grain of wood—a fault that makes them stand out prominently through any clear finish. For that reason, with dents covering a large area it is best either to patch them with a carefully matched piece of wood (see p. 50) or to grudgingly accept them as a feature that is part of the charm of the particular piece of furniture.

Wood Putty. Commercial wood putty is the best all-around material for filling cracks and blemishes. It is supplied in the form of a dry powder that is mixed with water. Wood putty can be sanded smooth. It should be applied to the stripped and washed piece before staining and filling.

Wood Dough. This is a generic term for products such as Plastic Wood. It is a mixture of powdered wood in a fast-drying plastic resin. It is strong and durable and can be sanded like wood. But it has serious drawbacks. The resin carrier has the nasty habit of penetrating the surrounding wood, effectively sealing it against stain and filler no matter how deeply the surface is sanded. It is also difficult to stain and should be stained very cautiously with a small brush to match it to the surrounding surface. In the final analysis, if it is used in fine finishing at all, it should be used in inconspicuous places or on pieces destined to be painted.

Lacquer Stick. This is the finisher's cure-all. It is excellent for filling small nail and screw holes and is widely used to touch up minor damage to finished furniture. If it is used before the final finish is applied, it should not be used until the piece has been stained and filled.

You can buy lacquer sticks from paint and finish suppliers and from movers' suppliers. They are rectangular sticks available in a wide range of colors to match virtually any finish. Lacquer stick is applied with a spatula or knife that has been heated over an alcohol lamp. The lacquer is melted onto the spatula and spread onto the wood like butter. The spatula is reheated and used to smooth the surface. As soon as the lacquer has cooled and hardened it can be sanded, but with skilled application very little sanding should be necessary.

Electrically heated spatulas can also be purchased. They avoid the problem of overheating the lacquer or having it cool before it reaches the surface. Suppliers also sell solvent-based "leveling agents" that can be wiped over the surface to smooth it without sanding.

Patches and Veneer Repairs

Deep dents and gouges in solid wood furniture and damaged areas on veneered pieces can be repaired inconspicuously by patching. This involves cutting out the damaged area and inserting a carefully matched piece of wood with the grain running the same way. Such repairs can be nearly invisible in a finished piece.

Veneer can be repaired on pieces that are not being refinished, but the patch must be carefully matched to the existing finish. The job is much easier on articles that are being completely refinished. Because removing finish usually involves water, which may loosen veneer, repairs to veneered pieces should be made after the old finish has been completely removed. To avoid loosening veneer during finishing, paint remover can be cleaned off with alcohol instead of water.

CUTTING A PATCH

Both types of repairs require the use of a template to cut a precisely matched hole and a piece to fit it. The edges of the patch should never run perpendicular to the grain but should cut across it at an angle. Seams of patches that run obliquely

Possible veneer patches.

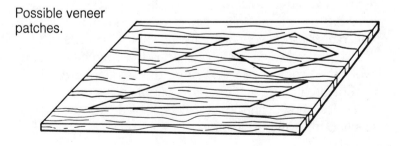

to the grain will be nearly invisible, those running perpen-dicular to it will show clearly. Common shapes for patches include diamonds, parallelograms, triangles, and other poly-gons. The proportions are not important. What is important is that the patch should be slightly larger than the damaged area and cover it completely. Edges may parallel the grain but must never cross it at a right angle. A few suppliers of specialized tools for fine woodworking offer veneer punches. These are similar to free-form cookie cutters and are used to punch out the damaged area and cut an identical replace-ment.

Veneer punches are not necessary to make a skillful patch, however. A template cut from light cardboard and a razor-sharp utility knife can be used to do a job that is every bit as good. Measure the size of the damaged area and design a patch that will cover all the bad wood. Draw the patch on the cardboard and cut out the pattern. Lay the resulting tem-plate over the damaged area and draw it carefully onto the damaged piece with either a sharp pencil or by scribing with the utility knife. If the patch is in veneer, peel out the dam-aged piece and clean all the old adhesive from the bottom of the hole with a sharp chisel.

If you are patching a solid piece of wood, it will be nec-essary to cut a "grave" into the damaged wood to accept the patch. Use a sharp chisel to hollow out the area inside the lines to a depth of $1/4$ to $3/8$ inch or even deeper if the damage extends further into the wood. Never use a hammer to drive a chisel. With the flat side of the chisel facing outward, press the blade into the wood precisely on the line. Then use the beveled side of the chisel to cut from about $1/4$ inch inside of the line down to the line at about a 45-degree angle. Keep the sides of the cut as nearly perpendicular as possible. When a straight-sided groove has been cut all the way around the edges of the patch, carefully guide the chisel with a thumb on the blade to provide pressure and control to cut away the wood inside the lines. Try to make the bottom of the "grave" as level as possible, although it need not be smooth—the irregularities will provide grip for the glue.

The key to a successful patching job, however, is not the hole but the piece that will be used to fill it. The patch should not only be of the same type of wood used in the original but should ideally be of the same age and have a similar grain pattern. And in some cases it may even be important to find wood that was sawn from the log in the same way. Oak, for example, shows a light wavy grain figure when it is cut "on the quarter." Quarter-sawn oak will not match oak cut in the conventional way or vice versa.

The ideal source of patches is the piece of furniture that is being repaired. Sometimes an inconspicuous piece of wood can be pirated to make a solid patch. The parting rails between drawers and doors are good places to look. Sometimes a piece can be cut from the inside of the skirt of a table. Be careful though. Often the structural wood in a piece of furniture is a different type, used because it is less expensive. And veneers are more difficult to find—they are almost never used in places that do not show.

If you can't find an inconspicuous piece of the article being repaired to use as a patch, the next best source is a broken piece of furniture of about the same age. Antique dealers frequently have broken parts of furniture in their storerooms and they are sometimes helpful. Another possibility is the town dump or the local junk dealer's. If all else fails, buy a new piece of the proper wood or veneer, although you will have to stain it carefully to match the older wood of the piece. Veneer can be obtained from specialty woodworking suppliers.

It is quite easy to remove veneer from old pieces of furniture for use in patching, especially if the old glue is loose. Remove any finish from the surface, then slide a sharp chisel, putty knife, or similar flat tool underneath the veneer and carefully peel it away from the surface. Rub the underside with steel wool to remove all the old glue. Store veneer between sheets of heavy paper with a weight on top to prevent it from curling.

INSTALLING PATCHES

Both veneer and solid patches are handled in the same way. Select an area that has a grain pattern close to the piece that was removed. Place the template on top of the patch—making absolutely sure that the grain runs exactly the same direction as it does across the hole that will accept the patch—and mark the edges. Cut the piece out as carefully as possible. Thin modern veneers can be cut with scissors although very fine-toothed veneer saws can also be used. Thicker patches should be cut flat through the face with a backsaw, the type of saw used in miter boxes.

Fit the patch carefully into its cavity. The fit should be as precise as possible. Rough edges can be cut down slightly with fine sandpaper and deep "graves" for solid patches may be trimmed judiciously with a small, sharp chisel. When a satisfactory fit has been achieved, apply a good glue to the bottom of the cavity. Set the patch into place and press it down gently. Cover the patch with a layer of waxed paper to prevent the glue that oozes from under the patch from sticking to the clamping blocks. Cover the waxed paper with a piece of thin cardboard to cushion the surface, place a flat block of wood on top of that, and then clamp it all firmly.

If the patch is located so clamping is not possible, a heavy weight will also work. A five-gallon can filled with water or sand makes a good weight. For curved surfaces, which are always tricky, a bag filled with sand can also be used as a clamp.

After the glue has set for at least 24 hours, remove the

clamps and sand the surface carefully with fine sandpaper, cutting away any glue that is on the surface and sanding the patch flush with the surrounding surface. If small gaps are apparent around the edge of the patch, they can be filled with lacquer stick after the finish has been applied. If the entire piece is being refinished, proceed. Otherwise stain, fill, and finish the patch and then apply a single coat of finish to the entire surface that contains the patch. After the finish has been rubbed down to its desired gloss, the patch should be almost invisible.

REMOVING VENEER BLISTERS

Moisture is the enemy of old veneer. A damp flowerpot or glass left on a veneered surface is likely to result in a blister. A thorough wetting and the entire surface may develop waves like the ocean. When an entire surface has become wavy, about the only solution is to remove the entire piece of veneer and replace it. Such large-scale repairs are beyond the scope of the amateur. They require the use of large veneer presses which can firmly clamp an entire surface. And even in cabinet shops, these are becoming scarce. Very little veneered furniture is now manufactured—most furniture companies now use lumber-core plywood in which the outer layer is a valuable cabinet wood. Edges are covered with veneer which is supplied on rolls and is extremely thin.

Blisters, however, can sometimes be repaired. They form because moisture has penetrated the veneer, softened the glue, and caused the veneer itself to swell. There is a long list of veneer-blister remedies among furniture finishers and few of them work. Some people say to apply steam, but that will only make the blister swell more. One effective way to repair a blister is to cut an X in it so that the resulting flaps can be laid flat. Trim the edges together where they overlap and reglue. Another method is to cut out the entire blister, soften the piece of veneer with water and then allow it to dry with a weight to hold it flat. Then the piece can be trimmed to fit the hole and glued back in place. Always handle the veneer gently. It is likely to be brittle and will crack easily. Never try to close a blister with pressure. It blistered because the veneer has expanded and become too big to fit the space intended for it.

RAISED VENEER ON EDGES

Sometimes veneer comes unglued near the edge of a surface. This can usually be corrected by working fresh glue under the veneer and clamping it tightly. Gently lift the veneer and scrape out as much accumulated dirt and old glue as possible with a flat, round-ended spatula. Since the old glue cannot be removed completely, try to use a glue that is similar to that used originally. If the piece was made prior to 1940, it is safe to assume that the veneer was secured with a water-soluble animal glue such as fish or hide glue. The best bet, then, is to use hide glue for repairs. With a spatula or a small piece of thin cardboard, work glue under the veneer and clamp it tightly for at least 24 hours.

3

Stripping

The single most important part of any wood finishing project is the proper preparation of the wood for the finish. No matter how carefully a final finish is applied or how high the quality of the finishing materials used, the hours of labor involved in applying a fine finish will be wasted and even the most painstakingly applied finish will look like a crude, inept job if shortcuts are taken at the outset. The resulting finish may be rough, may show uneven areas of coloration from pigments left in the wood, or may not adhere properly to the wood.

The prerequisites for a satisfactory finishing job are that the wood be sanded to satiny smoothness and, in the case of refinishing, that the wood be completely free of any former finishes or contamination. And that means completely, without a trace. Where old wood is concerned, restoring it to its former beauty or bringing out beauty that was never apparent with the original finish involves completely exposing the bare wood and bringing it to the same cleanliness and smoothness that it had upon leaving the cabinetmaker's shop when it was made.

Removing the Old Finish

When a piece is being refinished, the first step is the complete removal of all layers of previous finish. In some cases, though, it makes sense to attempt to restore an existing finish: if the finish is in salvageable condition or if the original finish is a major contributor to the value of the piece. An example is the handpainted and decorated European furniture from the eighteenth century. In some cases, the original finish accounts for nearly the entire value of the piece. This also holds true for some very old or rare museum-quality antiques. These latter rarely come into the hands of amateur refinishers.

For the most part, it is a matter of salvaging, and generally it's easier to apply a new finish than to try to restore badly aged or damaged finishes. Still, before plunging into paint remover, it can pay off to give a careful examination to the article you are about to start work on to determine its value and to decide whether minor repair of the existing finish will restore the piece to its former beauty. Restoration and repair of existing finishes is covered in Chapter 11.

Removing old finishes, or stripping, is probably what discourages the most people from taking up wood finishing or furniture refinishing as a hobby. And there is no doubt that it can be a messy, laborious job, because in the final analysis, there is no "paint remover" that removes paint, varnish, or any other finish; you do. Nonetheless, a basic knowledge of finishes and removers can make the task almost easy, and peeling off layers of paint and finish from a nondescript piece of furniture to expose richly grained wood (although if you don't check the wood first, you can peel layers of old paint to expose equally nondescript wood) can be one of the most gratifying parts of the whole finishing job.

About Finishes and Removers

Most old pieces of furniture were finished either with shellac or varnish. A few were originally painted, sometimes with the very tenacious "milk paints" (sometimes also known as refractory paints), and many were covered with coat after coat of paint over the years. Some newer pieces may also be painted with the recently developed finishes based on synthetic resins such as polyurethanes, acrylics, or latex, which are extremely difficult to remove.

COMMERCIAL PAINT AND VARNISH REMOVERS

Paint removers are combinations of solvents that will chemically weaken most finishes. They are capable of softening paints, varnishes, lacquers, and shellac. When properly used they will cut down to the bare wood and remove wood fillers from the pores of the grain as well. They will also partially remove wood stains, but for complete removal of these, bleaching is required.

While paint removers will remove most old finishes, some of the newer finishes are highly resistant to attack. Synthetic finishes such as urethanes, new types of varnish, latex paint, and milk paint can be difficult to remove with anything except the most powerful marine-type removers. And a few will not be affected by anything. The only way to find out, however, is to try. If regular paint remover does not do the job, try marine remover. If the finish resists that, methods such as heat or lye will have to be used.

Wax is added to some types of removers to retard evaporation, giving the remover a longer effective life. However, with wax-containing removers, all the wax must be washed from the wood before a finish can be applied. If any wax is present, most finishes will not adhere or cure properly.

Warning: Paint removers are toxic, although some are more dangerous than others. Some volatile solvents can burn the skin and are harmful if inhaled. They can also be absorbed through the skin. Most are extremely flammable.

When using paint removers treat them with respect. Avoid

contact with the skin (wearing rubber gloves can be a good idea) and work in areas with adequate ventilation so that fumes are dissipated, preferably outdoors. Never work near an open flame (don't forget the furnace and hot-water heater in the cellar). All but the most expensive removers based on methylene chloride are flammable, and high concentrations of fumes in the air can be explosive.

The common commercially available paint removers fall into six basic categories:

No-Wash Removers. These removers are the least expensive. They are almost always thin liquids that contain no wax and evaporate very quickly, but require no additional washing prior to applying a finish. They are frequently sold in large quantities to commercial strippers who use tanks or pumping apparatus for paint removal.

Liquid Removers. These do contain some wax, but because they are made from the most volatile solvents, they still tend to evaporate rather quickly. Their thin, runny consistency makes them difficult to use on vertical surfaces. However, their lack of body makes them invaluable for flushing finishes from carvings, fretwork, cracks, and other hard-to-get-at places. They are also useful for removing the last traces of finish: dip steel wool in remover and rub it over the tough spots.

Semipaste Removers. The addition of thickeners and the use of somewhat less volatile solvents makes semipaste removers the best all-purpose removers. They will cling to vertical surfaces better than the liquid types and have less tendency to spatter during application. They resist evaporation better than the liquids and, while they work somewhat more slowly, they remain active longer—so a single application will cut through more layers of finish.

Semipaste Marine Removers. If a finish resists other types of removers, marine-grade semipaste can be tried as a last resort before venturing on to more drastic methods. These are extremely powerful removers designed for tough varnishes and enamels. Their high price makes them impractical for day-to-day use.

Water-Washable Removers. These comparative newcomers are formulated so that the sludge that remains after they have done the job of softening the finish can be washed off with water. But while the idea of applying remover and then washing away the accumulated finish with a garden hose certainly seems attractive, they don't work quite that well. You still have to scrape and rub with steel wool, and they don't dissolve all that well in water. While they do combine stripping with the washing step to remove waxes, this benefit does not offset their high cost and unpleasant smell. Where they are useful is in a final cleanup where small areas of old finish are spotted on a piece that has already been stripped and washed free of wax. They can be used here for spot removing and washed away without contaminating the area with wax.

Paste Removers. These are very expensive, special-purpose removers that can be used on overhead areas without dripping. They are often custom formulated and have little use in furniture refinishing.

Using Commercial Finish Removers

Before starting to strip, select a space in which to work. Any way you do it, it is a messy business. Be sure to have enough room to work and ample provision for getting rid of finish sludge. By far the best place to remove finishes from furniture is outdoors. You won't have to worry about ventilation and, unless you are careless with cigarettes, the fire hazard will be minimal. For working outdoors, calm, warm days when the temperature is above 70° F are the best. Removers work better at moderate temperatures. Direct sunlight should be avoided, because it may cause the remover to evaporate too rapidly. Work in a place sheltered from the wind to further reduce evaporation. Also, humid days are better than dry ones.

If the work must be done inside, much greater care will have to be exercised to prevent getting sludge and paint remover on things that you would just as soon keep the finish on. A garage with a floor drain is about the best indoor location, followed by a basement workshop. But in a basement be sure ventilation is adequate and beware of open flames in water heaters and furnaces.

Set up for work by getting all the materials that you will need before you apply any remover. You will need paint remover, a small can or jar, coarse steel-wool pads, soft cloths, a wide-bladed putty knife, an old paint brush, denatured alcohol, and an ample supply of old newspapers. Always keep a pail of water nearby; if you spatter remover on yourself, wash it off immediately. Wear old clothes and use rubber or canvas gloves to protect your hands.

WORKING WITH FINISH REMOVERS

When everything is ready, finish remover can be applied. Place a small quantity of remover in a jar or tin can and reseal the remover container to prevent evaporation while you work.

Using an old or inexpensive natural-bristle paintbrush (once a brush has been in remover it is not good for much else), flow on a thick coat of remover, brushing in one direction only. The object is to get as much remover onto the wood as possible; brushing back and forth as in painting will only thin out the coating.

Don't try to cover the entire piece with remover in one application. You won't be able to work fast enough, and if the remover dries out, the finish will harden right back again. Rather, select an area of no more than 2 to 3 square feet. If the piece is small enough to be turned, strip one surface at a time, always working on a horizontal surface if possible.

After applying a thick coating of remover, be patient and let the remover do as much of the job as it can. If it doesn't seem to be working fast enough, don't brush over it—stirring it up will not make it work faster but instead will disturb the protective film of wax that has formed on the surface and allow faster evaporation of the solvents. Wait about 10 minutes and then take a look at the finish. If the remover has started to disintegrate it, paint will have blistered and wrinkled, while shellac and lacquer will have become a viscous mass. Take your broad knife or a putty knife and scrape it gently across the surface to see if the remover has penetrated all the way to wood. If not, wait another 10 minutes and try again.

If the finish still has not softened down to the wood after 20 minutes, flow more remover onto the surface. This will replace solvents that have been lost through evaporation and allow the remover to go on working without drying up. Repeat the same procedure, checking it at 10-minute intervals. If that still doesn't penetrate to the wood, the piece either has an extremely thick coating of finish or you have hit a layer of something that is obstinate. In either case, scrape off the softened finish to expose the resistant layers and test a spot with remover to see if it will soften the finish. If it works, cover the whole area and let it work until it gets to the bottom of it all. If the finish seems to be unfazed by the remover you are using, test an area with a stronger marine-grade remover. And if that still doesn't do the job, you'll have to resort to some of the stronger measures outlined in later sections.

When the remover has softened the finish all the way to the wood, scrape off the softened paint. Hold the scraper or knife so that the blade leans toward you at about a 60-degree angle. Always pull toward yourself in smooth gentle strokes to avoid gouging or scratching the wood. Don't try to take the finish off completely by scraping because it is too easy to damage the wood with the scraping tool and you will only have to repair any damage you do at this stage later on. Scrape the finish sludge onto newspapers.

Warning: Allow the residue to dry before disposing of the papers—it is very flammable, and spontaneous combustion can occur. Once dry, dispose of the paper carefully in sealed garbage cans; it is still very flammable.

To remove the residue that is left after scraping off the heavy part of the finish, rub with coarse steel-wool pads that have been dipped in remover. Stubborn spots may require another application of remover. Clean remover and softened paint out of carvings, moldings, and turnings with the tip of a dull paring knife, but be very careful not to gouge the wood. Sharpened wooden tools such as dowels that are cut at a 45-degree angle, Popsicle sticks, and wooden or bamboo skewers also work well and are less likely to harm the wood. A handy trick for cleaning finish out of the narrow sections of turnings like chair rungs is to dip a length of rough hemp or sisal rope in remover and pull it through the groove with a sawing motion.

WASHING OUT THE REMOVER

After removing the finish from the entire piece, a thorough washdown is required to remove any residue of wax left by the remover. One method is to flush the surface with a solvent such as denatured alcohol or turpentine. Don't skimp on this step—any wax left on the wood will prevent most finishes from adhering properly or drying: the only recourse will be to strip the piece and start all over. Lacquer, for example, is particularly sensitive to the presence of wax. Flush the surface of the wood thoroughly and mop up with soft cloths, repeating several times. Work quickly to avoid letting the solvent evaporate, or the dissolved wax will only be redeposited on the wood.

A more effective washing solution, particularly when the piece is to be bleached, filled, and stained, is trisodium phosphate. This chemical, which is a mild remover in its own right and is often used to remove varnish from floors, is sold in paint stores as TSP or under the tradename Mex. Chemically, it is an alkali, although not nearly as strong as lye. While exposure to concentrated solutions can burn the skin, in the dilutions used in finish removal it is far less irritating than most paint removers. TSP is very inexpensive and is by far the most economical remover for large jobs such as floors. It is simply dissolved in very hot water, one pound in a six-quart pail, and mopped onto the floor. The finish will disintegrate without becoming gummy as with solvent-based removers and can be taken off by vigorous scrubbing or steel wool. The finish is mopped up with clear water.

When a solution of TSP is used as a wash following the use of solvent-type removers, it foams on contact with the softened paint and remover and washes both away without a trace. It will take off the wax from the remover, remove final traces of filler from the pores of the wood, take out a good part of the stains in the wood, and partially bleach the wood. In addition, it opens the pores of the wood so that bleaching solutions penetrate more readily. Because TSP opens the pores, it may roughen the surface of the wood somewhat. This roughness is easily removed by sanding. Care should also be exercised when using TSP on veneered surfaces (see p. 66).

To use TSP as a post-remover wash, add one cup of TSP to about ⅔ of a pail of very hot water. A good time to mix the washing solution is while the remover is working. After the remover has softened the finish down to the wood, scrape off the heavy sludge (if the finish is thin, washing will take it off and scraping can be skipped). Apply the hot TSP solution with a scrub brush. When the TSP comes into contact with the wet remover and softened finish, it will form suds in a vigorous reaction that will seem to boil the old finish off the wood. Scrub and apply the TSP liberally until the suds cease to be discolored by the finish and are nearly white. Then wash with clear water, wipe off the excess with a soft cloth, and set the piece aside to dry, out of the sun.

While the piece is still damp from washing, clean corners and carvings of any residue with a dull paring knife or wooden tools. Be very careful not to gouge the wood; it is softer when it's wet. Keep an eye on the piece while it is drying—areas that are not completely free of old finish will begin to show up. Very small spots can usually be cleaned up with steel wool and water, larger areas may require a second application of remover (water-washable removers work well for this purpose because they don't need to be followed by a TSP wash).

If the piece is to be bleached, it need not be completely dry. Otherwise allow it to dry completely. In dry weather this will require at least 48 hours, but wait longer if you can. Excessive moisture in the wood can cause warping after the finish has been applied.

USING REMOVERS ON STUBBORN FINISHES

Some enamels and all latex paints are very resistant to finish removers. Even with the powerful marine-type removers it may be possible to soften only one coat of enamel at a time. And latex paints hold the record for being the most remover-resistant coating ever devised for wood. While specially formulated removers claiming to do the job are on the market, most fall far below expectation.

In these cases, finish removal can sometimes be made easier by covering the wet remover with water-soaked newspapers or burlap. This will slow the evaporation rate of the solvents in the remover and, if the covering is kept wet, the remover will work for as long as 8 hours. The results can often be very satisfactory and it is a good technique to try before resorting to caustics or torches.

Another frequently encountered problem is paint in the pores of the wood. It is very difficult to remove and frequently remains even after stripping and washing with TSP. This gives the wood a speckled appearance, with each pore showing a tiny dot of color. About the only way to get it out is to use a liquid paint remover and scrub over it with a stiff brush. This will usually float all or most of the buried paint out of the pores. If a faint residue is left, it can be hidden by subsequent application of a wood filler.

STRIPPING VENEER, INLAY, AND PLASTER OF PARIS

A word about veneer is in order here. The problem with stripping veneered antique furniture is that even the finest veneers were put on with water-soluble glues. As a result, prolonged exposure to water will cause them to lift and blister. Large pieces of veneer—a tabletop or dresser, for example— are not usually threatened by normal stripping, although care should be taken in the washing step to avoid unnecessarily long exposure to water, and the piece should be allowed to dry thoroughly before further work is attempted.

Furniture with veneer inlay or marquetry does present a problem, however. The small pieces of veneer used to make a design or decorative border are very sensitive to moisture, and if they become loosened, repair is a painstaking and arduous task. The job of stripping an inlaid piece of furniture is made easier because the workmanship is so fine that few of these pieces have been covered with coat upon coat of paint. Therefore, there is not a very great risk of discovering inlay when it is already too late.

With inlay, care should be taken to minimize contact with water. Wash it with a solvent like alcohol instead of TSP. Damage to inlay can be avoided by removing the finish one coat at a time. Apply a thin coat of remover (the liquid types will let you watch the remover's progress more closely), give it a few minutes to work, and wipe (do not scrape!) the remover and finish off with fine steel wool. Let the area dry completely, then repeat as many times as necessary. Finally, wash down the area with alcohol, using a soft cloth to mop the inlay as dry as possible.

A similar problem is sometimes presented by the discovery that "carvings" or fretwork on a piece of furniture are not wood at all but are made from plaster of paris. Applied decorative details of this type are quite common on mass-produced furniture from the 1930s. While they are not as delicate as inlaid veneer, care in stripping is advisable. The problem is that they are softened both by remover and by washing, and can be easily damaged if treated roughly while soft. Also, because plaster is so absorbent it conducts moisture to the glue that attaches the carvings to the piece, they can come unglued quite easily.

There is a way to avoid losing or damaging plaster-of-paris appliqués. First use paint remover, and be very careful when scraping finish out of the crevices. Carefully wash the remover off the plaster with alcohol. Then allow the piece to dry completely. After the "carving" has dried, proceed with stripping the flat surfaces of the piece and wash with TSP. While all that may seem fairly complicated, the job is made much easier by the fact that most of the furniture made with applied plaster decoration was finished with shellac which is very easy to remove.

Care is also in order when stripping applied carvings made

from wood. If they get too moist, the glue will soften and they will have to be reglued, which is something that's easier avoided than done. In addition, they may warp so badly as to be impossible to reglue.

STRIPPING HARDWARE

If the hardware has been covered with finish over the years, place it in a glass jar with a small amount of remover in the bottom (there is no need to cover the hardware, the fumes from the remover will do the work). Seal the jar to prevent the fumes from escaping and set it aside. When you have some spare time (the remover will usually do its work in a few hours, but hardware can be left in a sealed jar with remover almost indefinitely), wash off the softened finish with hot water and detergent, using a small stiff brush like a toothbrush to clean out recessed areas. Polish the hardware with a good metal polish that will not leave a residue. Always wear gloves when polishing hardware; the acid from your fingers will tarnish brass and copper almost immediately. To protect it from tarnishing, place the hardware on a piece of newspaper or cardboard and spray it with a clear protective metal lacquer. The kind sold in automotive-supply stores works best.

Removing Finishes with Lye

The mere suggestion of using lye to remove finishes will cause many people who work with wood and furniture to look at you with horror. If they don't walk away shaking their heads in disgust, you may be in for a lecture on the proper respect that should be shown to wood. For lye is the most controversial finish remover, and virtually everyone has a strong opinion about its use. Yet it is widely used and in many cases it may make the difference between successfully stripping a piece of furniture or giving up in despair.

Warning: Lye is the most dangerous chemical sold openly in stores. It is extremely caustic and will severely burn the skin every bit as rapidly as it will cut through layers of paint and finish that shrug off the most powerful commercial removers. Unless it is flushed off immediately with cold water, permanent burns can occur.

Lye, however, can be used safely and finishes can be removed from wood without destroying either the wood or the furniture. The object, of course, is to remove the finish but to stop the action of the lye before it has much time to attack the wood. A common objection to lye is that it burns the wood. It does not "burn" the wood but it does discolor it, and any lye-stripping job will affect the color of the wood. As a general rule, it darkens any wood, but it affects some woods more than others. With pine and some other light-colored woods (maple, oak, and birch, for example), the result is a warm honey color that many people find desirable. When they find it on old pieces, they value it and refer to it as "patina." Its effect on dark, open-grained woods, including walnut and mahogany, is to turn them very dark. In these cases, the wood can be easily returned to its natural color by bleaching (see Chapter 4).

Another effect that lye has on wood should be noted. It raises the grain and opens the pores of the wood. When the piece is still wet after stripping, the wood may present a rough, rather punky surface. Much of the roughness will disappear as the piece dries, and the surface can be easily returned to its original smoothness by sanding. With open-grained woods where fillers are going to be used (oak, for example), the effect of opening the pores can be an advantage, making the wood accept filler more readily.

Nonetheless, lye should never be used on veneer. Before

you begin to strip a piece of furniture with lye, scrape the finish away from an edge and determine if the piece is veneered. The caustic action of the lye solution will cause almost any veneer to blister or wrinkle, and in many cases, to peel off completely.

Also, avoid using lye on pieces with press carving. This is decorative carving that is frequently found on kitchen chairs and other furniture made in the early part of the twentieth century. It was done by placing soaked wood in a heavy press that compressed the wood to give the appearance of carving. As long as the wood is dry, the carved appearance will remain. But prolonged exposure to water, and consequently exposure to lye solution, will cause the grain to swell and revert to its natural position, with the result that the carving will be lost. Bentwood furniture presents a similar problem and should not be stripped with lye either. The furniture was made by bending soaked or steamed wood, which retained that shape after it dried. When it is wet with lye solution, the wood will relax and try to return to its original straight position. This may cause it to split.

Because of its drawbacks and limitations, lye is recommended only when commercial removers will not do the job. In cases where a piece of furniture is covered with layer upon layer of tough, remover-resistant paint, lye can reduce an almost impossible job to a matter of minutes. In fact, the main problem with working with lye is not getting it to attack the paint but controlling its action so that it destroys the old finish without undue damage to the wood. To work properly, a strong solution is required; a weak solution does not slow down the action, it just doesn't work at all. As a result, the way to use lye is to cover a single surface of the furniture, let it sit a short time, scrub it off, taking any weakened paint along with it, and repeat until all the finish is removed.

An ample supply of water is mandatory when working with lye solutions. The best place to work is outside, with a running garden hose, although several buckets of cold water could also be used. The water is used to wash the lye off the wood as the softened paint is scraped away and to immediately remove any lye you may splash on yourself. While it is possible to strip furniture with lye in a basement with a floor drain, be prepared to make a mess. And if you have a painted floor, forget it. Assuming that the job can be done outside, wait for a hot day. The temperature must be above 65° F, but the higher the temperature, the better lye will work. Also, select a place where no grass is growing or a place where you don't care if the grass is killed.

When stripping with lye, always wear old clothing or even protective clothing. At least wear long sleeves and rubber gloves. Goggles are a good idea as well. Mix the lye solution in a galvanized steel or plastic pail. Never use an aluminum container—lye reacts with aluminum and will destroy it while releasing a lot of noxious fumes. To a pail half full of hot water add ⅓ to ½ can (they are usually 13 ounces) of lye, which is sold under a variety of trade names in grocery stores for clearing plugged drains. Pour the lye *slowly* into the water; never add water to dry lye—it will react violently and may spatter on you or boil out of the container. The lye will dissolve in the water easily and generate a considerable amount of heat in the process. The solution may boil and will foam a great deal, so keep your eyes and hands out of the way. When the lye is completely dissolved the solution will be very hot.

Apply the lye solution to a single surface of the furniture at a time. It is so caustic that it will dissolve most paint brushes, so most professional strippers use a cheap scrub brush. Long-handled cotton dish mops of the kind sold in supermarkets also work quite well. Scrub the lye onto the surface of the wood. Since lye is very runny, try to minimize the amount that will drip into other parts of the piece. Let the lye work for a minute or two. Unlike removers, there will be no blistering or wrinkling to show that the lye is attacking the finish. Rather than softening the finish, lye causes it to disintegrate into a powder. Wash away the lye by turning the hose on the piece or by using a scrub brush and buckets of water. Scrub vigorously with the brush until all the loosened paint has been removed. By repeating this procedure and taking the finish off a layer at a time it is possible to limit the contact of lye with bare wood.

As usual, though, there are problems. In this case it is turnings for legs, carvings, and other cracks and crevices. Stripping case-goods, like dressers, with lye can be relatively simple, but a piece with lots of crevices filled with paint is more difficult. The problem is that paint will collect in the cracks and will be much thicker there than on flat surfaces. So when the flat areas are clear of paint there will still be paint in the crevices.

One way to overcome this problem is to try commercial removers at this point. The lye will have weakened the paint enough so that removers will be able to finish the job. Another trick that is sometimes used is to mix a cup of wheat-based wallpaper paste with two quarts of lye solution. This will make a paste that can be applied to small vertical areas without running onto the bare wood.

After the old finish and most of the lye have been removed by scrubbing and water, it is still necessary to neutralize any lye that may have penetrated into the wood. This is accomplished with distilled white vinegar, which is a mild acid. Apply the vinegar freely, taking particular care to let it run into any cracks or crevices where lye could have accumulated. There is no need to wash off the vinegar; leave it on the wood and it will evaporate as the piece dries.

When furniture has been stripped with lye, it is very wet because of the large amounts of water used and because the lye has increased the porosity of the wood. Complete drying is extremely important: let it dry for at least three days either indoors or outside. But don't try to hurry the drying by placing the piece in direct sunlight—too much direct heat can cause warping.

Removing Finishes with Heat

Like lye, the idea of taking the finish off a piece of fine furniture with an open flame causes a great deal of consternation. According to a surprising number of experts in the field, it is all right for porch steps and the sides of houses but has no place in furniture refinishing. Yet a torch can be one of the fastest, safest ways to remove thick coats of paint from a piece of furniture, and with a little care, the danger of damaging the piece is no greater than that of gouging the surface while scraping off paint-remover sludge.

PROPANE TORCH

The secret to using a torch is simply not to go too fast. Even taking your time and working slowly, it is possible to remove a thick accumulation of old paint in less time, and at less expense, than with removers. While removing the paint from a dresser that has been coated with many layers of paint may take 4 or 5 hours with remover, the job can be done with a torch in an hour or less. The common objection to using a torch is that the wood will be scorched, leaving deep, darkened scars that will have to be sanded off and will permanently ruin the appearance of the piece. But in order to burn the wood, the paint will have to be burned first, and the object in this case is not to *burn* off the paint but to soften it with heat so that it can be easily scraped off. If you apply only enough heat to wrinkle and loosen the paint without scorching it, there is no danger of burning or scorching the wood. In fact the heavy layers of paint will insulate the wood so that even slight scorching of the paint will not affect the wood.

The technique is simple. Use a torch to strip only those pieces of furniture or wood that are very thickly coated with paint or latex paints that do not respond well to removers. Never try to use a torch to remove clear finishes—they are so thin that it is almost impossible to soften the finish without harming the wood. The only tools required are a small propane torch and a right-angle scraper. These scrapers have a blade set at a right angle to the handle and are available in paint and hardware stores. Hold the torch far enough from the paint so that the paint begins to blister after a minute or so but not so close that the paint scorches. Work on a small area at a time, about 3 inches square, and move the torch constantly to avoid heating any spot too much. When the paint has blistered and is soft, scrape it off and proceed to a new area. Start at any inside corner where the heaviest accumulations of paint are located.

Do not try to clean the wood completely with the torch. As the paint is removed, so is the protection that it gives the wood. If small areas do not come off, leave them and go on. In other words, soften and remove as much of the paint as

Scrapers of the type shown here are the best for removing softened paint.

can be easily done with one pass by the torch, leaving tough spots and a thin film of paint on the wood.

As usual, carvings and the crevices formed by moldings are the most difficult areas. Heat the paint in the same way but use a stiff wire brush instead of a scraper. Take off only the paint that comes easily—rarely will it be possible to get out all, or even most, of the paint this way. But don't try to reheat it to loosen more of the paint. You will only increase the risk of scorching the wood, and sanding scorches off of carvings is just about impossible to do successfully.

When all the paint that can be easily softened with the torch has been scraped off, remove the remaining residue with a good semipaste remover. The torch should have taken off enough of the paint so that one coat of remover will take it down to the bare wood without any problem. By following the heat from a torch with solvent removers and TSP, it should be possible to take a thickly coated piece of furniture or wood paneling down to the bare wood with a minimum of heartache and without any damage to the wood itself.

That old standby, the gasoline blowtorch, should be avoided. It is much more dangerous to use than the inexpensive propane torches and much harder to control. It is largely because of the blowtorch that using heat to remove paint has such a bad reputation; fortunately, it has been made all but obsolete by the propane torch.

HEATED SCRAPERS AND HEAT GUNS

A mention of heated electrical paint-removing devices is appropriate here. These are available in several forms, the most common of which is a flat heated surface combined with a scraper. The paint is softened by contact with the heated plate and then removed by scraping. Their advertising claims that they are safer than an open flame. This is no doubt true, but they are also much less effective at removing paint. They don't get hot enough to do much of a job at softening the paint, and because their heated surface is brought in contact with the paint, they get gummed up with softened paint and generally make a smoky mess.

On the other hand, industrial heat guns do quite a good job. These resemble hand-held blowers, except that they put out a blast of air that has been heated to temperatures between 350° and 1000° F. As with a torch, you simply direct the heat at the paint, wait for it to soften, and scrape it off. While they are not quite as hot as a torch, the heat is more easily controlled and the danger of burning the wood is even less. Their main drawback is that they are quite expensive. They have recently become available from suppliers of wood-finishing materials.

Removing Milk Paints

Milk paints, sometimes also known as refractory paints, are beyond a doubt the most difficult to remove of any wood-finishing material ever devised. And that is no exaggeration. They are unaffected by the strongest solvent-based commercial removers, are resistant to caustic solutions such as lye, and simply turn brown and burn without lifting when exposed to the heat of a torch. They are usually found on homemade furniture and old farmhouse paneling or wainscoting and are almost always the first coat of finish ever put on the wood.

Like the furniture and woodwork that they are found on, they are homemade paints, usually made by farmers in places where oil-based paints and finishes were prohibitively expensive or unavailable. They were made by mixing spoiled milk or buttermilk with locally available pigments like berry juices, rust, lamp-black (which is just very fine soot), or animal blood. They are almost always red, black, green, or brown and tend to be pale, pastel shades.

While mixing milk with a natural pigment does not sound like much, they are incredibly durable paints. In fact, the red paint originally used on barns was milk paint colored with animal blood, and barns can be found where it has not completely weathered away after one hundred years or more. The reason is that milk paints penetrate very deeply into the wood, so deeply in fact that sanding them off is hopeless: they are chemically the same as the milk or casein glues. The easiest way to tell if you have a piece of furniture that has been coated with milk paint is that, if it doesn't come off, the odds are that it is milk paint. On furniture, milk paints are found most frequently on pieces made from pine and having the simple functional design of furniture made by a man for his own home, although they are sometimes found on pieces made from better woods and even on some that were obviously made by professional furniture makers.

The easiest way out of the milk paint problem is to leave it on and restore it. Strip off the other coats of finish (you won't have to worry about hurting the milk paint), sand the surface smooth, mix up a batch of milk paint of the same color, and recoat the piece. All you need is powdered milk, mixed to double strength, and some dry pigments of the type sold in good paint and art-supply stores.

If you insist on finishing the piece your way, milk paint can be removed, but it is neither easy nor pleasant. About the only thing that will touch it is ammonia. Household ammonia of the type sold in grocery stores will work but it is a weak solution; commercial ammonia, on the other hand, is much stronger but is also fairly dangerous to work with and is more difficult to obtain. While ammonia solutions are considered to be fairly weak as bases go, even household ammonia can be very rough on the hands, and the fumes are noxious to say the least. They will cause eyes to water and sting, and if they are inhaled, choking and coughing result. Needless to say, wear rubber gloves, work in a very well-ventilated place, and try not to breathe too much of the fumes.

The procedure requires a fair amount of elbow grease. Dip medium-grade steel wool into either household or commercial ammonia and scrub it into the surface of the paint, wetting the whole surface. Keep going over it, keeping the surface constantly wet with ammonia. This is important, because those fumes coming off are the ammonia evaporating out of the solution, so the longer it's on the wood, the weaker it's getting. When it stops smelling, all that's on the wood is water. So keep scrubbing and keep adding new ammonia, and in about 10 minutes, if you're lucky, it should start to soften the paint. The paint will turn to a viscous, gooey mass that will come off in the steel wool. When the steel wool gets clogged with paint, start on a new pad, and keep going until all the paint has been removed.

After all the paint has come off, rinse the piece with clear water and let it dry. Like lye, ammonia has a darkening effect on the wood, which in some cases can be attractive and in others may require bleaching to restore the wood to its former natural color. If you bleach, it can be done immediately, before the piece is set out to dry. Since the wood has been soaked with water, allow at least three days for drying before proceeding.

Even though ammonia will take off milk paints, some pigment may remain buried in the wood no matter how diligently you rub with steel wool and how much ammonia you use. In some cases, this faint coloration may be desirable or it can be masked by staining later on. One pigment that is particularly stubborn is black; even bleaching will not lighten it. If it is too dark for a clear finish, a coat of black enamel is the best alternative.

Commercial Furniture Strippers

In the early sixties, just about anyone looking for a business to get into went into furniture stripping, and for a while it seemed that there would soon be a furniture-stripping shop on every street corner. It is perfectly fair to say that a lot of these people didn't know what they were doing. Many used tanks filled with heated lye, some used blasts of live steam, and many pieces of fine furniture were ruined or came out looking like the side of a two-hundred-year-old barn.

Things have settled down quite a bit since then, and there are now many strippers that do very acceptable work. New mixtures of chemicals have become available that take off the paint or finish without harming or discoloring the wood. As a result, commercial strippers are now a viable alternative for the apartment dweller with no work space or for the person with an interest in finishing wood who finds the gratification of exposing wood that has been covered with thick coats of finish somewhat elusive. While their prices vary quite widely and they are certainly far more expensive than the investment in materials and tools for a stripping job, they are generally quite economical if the labor in the project is considered.

Since there are still some "wood butchers" around that somehow manage to stay in business, there are a few things that should be noted before trusting a potentially good piece of furniture to a stripper. The easiest way to evaluate the quality of his work is to ask to see a piece that he has stripped. Because of the large number of crevices, glue joints, and hard-to-get-at surfaces on a chair, examining a chair is one of the best ways to evaluate the quality of workmanship that you can expect. First take a look at the wood. The surface should be smooth (although not necessarily as smooth as fine sanding will make it) and the grain not raised and roughened too much. The color should be a natural color for that wood, or at least not unduly whitened or darkened or stained from the stripping process. This, of course, is somewhat subjective. Almost any stripping operation will raise the grain of the wood to some degree and affect the color somewhat. In addition, different wood will respond in different ways. The effect is the least pronounced on close-grained woods like maple and the most apparent on open-grained woods such as oak. If you can look at a piece of oak that has been stripped and see that the grain is not overly raised, you can be assured that the process will not harm the wood.

Next, examine the crevices formed by the turnings on the legs and the joints where the back meets the seat. Look for any paint or traces of finish in these areas. They are most difficult places to strip because they are places where finish accumulates. They should be completely free of finish. Also, wiggle the chair to see if the glue joints have been weakened or loosened. For this, you might have to check a couple of pieces, because you will have no way of knowing if the glue joints were loose before stripping. If most of the pieces you look at seem to have weak glue joints, find another stripper. And be very careful of veneer, the most delicate glue problem of all. Some strippers can do veneered pieces without loosening or destroying the veneer, but many cannot. Before leaving a piece for stripping, find out whether or not it is veneered by scraping off some of the old finish on an edge to expose the seam between the veneer and the base wood. If it is veneered, ask to look at some veneered pieces that he has stripped and check very carefully to be sure the veneer has not wrinkled or lifted. And make sure the stripper knows that the piece is veneered and treats it accordingly.

4

Chemical Changes: Bleaching and Aging Wood

Most operations in wood finishing do not actually alter the chemistry of the wood. The exceptions are bleaching wood to remove its natural color and treating wood with acid to even out unruly grain and enhance its response to stains.

Bleaches are also used to remove residual stain from wood that has resisted the action of paint removers. In addition, they are used to remove spots and discoloration that remain in the wood and would be visible through a finish.

By removing oils and resin from the wood, acid treatment mimics that natural aging process of wood. It is especially useful on new pine—in particular unfinished furniture. New pine accepts stain in a very uneven manner because it has broad bands of grain that are far less porous than the adjoining wood. Even the honey-colored stains used on pine cannot come anywhere near reproducing the uniform mellow tones of old pine. But by increasing the porosity of the wood by treating it with acid, the "old pine" appearance can be closely approximated.

Bleaching and Removing Stubborn Stains

If stripping is done with conventional removers followed by a wash with trisodium phosphate (TSP), in most cases the wood is left completely clean of old stain and wood fillers. This also holds true with caustics like lye. But if no-wash or liquid removers are used by themselves, a residue of stain and filler may remain in the wood. And occasionally even washing with TSP is not sufficient to remove some stubborn stains that have been applied to early furniture.

There are cases where stains are so tenacious and have penetrated so deeply into the wood they can be removed only by sanding away half the piece, but in most cases they can be removed by bleaching the wood after stripping. It may seem to make more sense to leave them in the wood and proceed with the finishing job, yet the finest finishes are those in which the refinisher starts with wood that has been restored to its original state of cleanliness.

Besides removing traces of stain from wood, there are two other cases in which wood may be bleached. Wood that has been chemically darkened by stripping, particularly wood that has been stripped with lye, can be restored to its natural color. And all natural color can be bleached out of wood if you want to apply a blond finish.

Bleaching to Remove Residual Color

If old pieces of wood or furniture still show signs of color from stain or fillers in the pores or grain, they should be bleached. In this case the most effective, simplest, and cheapest method is to use commercial laundry bleach. Choose any brand—from Clorox on, they are all sodium hypochlorite in water and are all the same concentration.

Since the bleach must penetrate the wood to get at stains that have penetrated the surface of the wood, it is essential that the surface of the wood be perfectly clean and free of old finish, sealers, oil, grease, or glue. To be sure that the wood is free from all materials that could protect it from the bleach, old wood should be washed with a solution of TSP (see p. 64 for a description of this procedure) before the bleach is applied.

To bleach, simply flood the surface of the wood with laundry bleach at full strength. Use an old rag, a sponge, or a cheap paintbrush. Keep the surface of the wood wet with bleach for about 5 minutes, then either wash off the bleach with clear water or neutralize it with a half-strength solution of white vinegar. Let the piece dry for at least a couple of days; it must be thoroughly dry before you proceed.

In most cases, laundry bleach will remove stains and coloration that have survived stripping. The two exceptions are lampblack and red stains that were made from berry juice. In antique furniture, lampblack was sometimes rubbed into the wood as part of a fake graining process. The object was to make one wood look like another. With some antiques, especially those made from mahogany, a pinkish red stain occasionally remains after stripping. This may or may not be berry juice and there is only one way to tell: apply bleach. If it won't come out, then it's berry juice.

Bleaching to Remove the Natural Color of the Wood

Such stains as berry juice can be removed with commercial wood bleaches, though. These solutions are so strong, however, that they are usually used primarily to remove the natural color of the wood, leaving it a grayish-white that looks rather like driftwood. This is done when the wood is to be finished with a blond finish (which was quite popular for a while) or when the finisher wishes to "start from scratch" by staining the exact color desired.

This type of bleaching involves solutions that have stronger bleaching action than laundry bleach. The bleaches that will remove the natural color from wood are oxalic acid and commercially available two-solution wood bleaches.

BLEACHING WITH OXALIC ACID

Oxalic acid is a strong bleach that, despite its somewhat scary name, is not caustic in contact with the skin. It can be used in wood finishing to remove the natural color from wood. It will also remove residual stains from wood, is about the only bleach that will take out black water stains, rust stains, and will lighten chemically darkened wood. (Black stains occur when wood is soaked with water and then dries slowly. They are found in old furniture that has been exposed to the elements or where moisture from a wet object like a glass has penetrated finish, and on lumber that has been stacked outdoors.) Oxalic acid will also lighten wood that has been chemically darkened by stripping with lye or ammonia.

When oxalic acid is used to remove stains from wood or to lighten chemically darkened wood, it is important to stop the bleaching action at the proper moment. If bleaching progresses too far, the natural color will be removed from the wood. However, if you do remove more of the color than you had intended, all is not lost—the reaction can be reversed. With wood, bleaches will remove color; stains can put it back.

Oxalic acid can be purchased at drugstores or large paint stores. Since the type sold in drug stores is intended for medical use, it is of high purity and much more expensive than that sold through industrial outlets. In either case, it is used in a saturated solution that gives maximum strength. To prepare a solution of oxalic acid, mix about 3 ounces of acid crystals into 1 quart of hot tap water.

While oxalic acid can be used by itself as a bleach, its effectiveness is greatly enhanced if it is used with a second solution of sodium hyposulfite. This is simply photographic hypo and can be obtained in any photographic-supply store. For the purpose of bleaching wood, a solution prepared by adding 3 ounces of crystals to 1 quart of hot water is best.

To bleach with oxalic acid, use an old rag or paintbrush, flushing the surface of the wood with the oxalic-acid solution. Check carefully to be sure all areas are wet with the solution—if you notice spots that seem to be drying faster than other areas, old finish or some other obstacle to the penetration of the solution is probably present. Clean it up with steel wool. When you are sure that all the wood is soaked with the first solution, cover the surface with the solution of hypo.

Let the solution sit for about half an hour or until it has reached the desired lightness. If it is still too dark after that time, apply more oxalic acid and follow it with more hypo. When the desired degree of lightness has been reached, stop its bleaching action by washing the surface with white vinegar. Let it sit for a minute or two and then wash well with clear water. It is important to wash off all the oxalic acid—when it dries it will form a powder that is extremely irritating to the nose and mouth. This dust can make subsequent sanding a very unpleasant operation. Let the wood dry for at least 24 hours before proceeding.

USING TWO-SOLUTION BLEACHES

The most effective, and strongest, bleaches for removing the natural color of wood are commercial bleaches that are available at paint stores. There are a few brands, but most consist of two solutions that are applied one at a time to the wood. The wood is coated evenly with the first solution, it is allowed a few minutes to penetrate, and the second solution is applied. Bleaching then takes place over the next few hours. While most manufacturers claim that no neutralizing is necessary, washing the surface with white vinegar after applying these bleaches cannot hurt, and you make sure that no active bleach is left in the wood to harm subsequent stain and finish coats.

Two-solution bleaches will remove all the natural color from the wood. When they are applied to walnut, for instance, the final color will be a light tan. Because of their potency, they should be used with care and the instructions provided with the bleach followed closely. Some are fairly dangerous: wear protective clothing and rubber gloves, and avoid contact with the mouth and eyes.

Removing Stains and Discoloration

Frequently, old pieces of furniture will have been stained and discolored by use. Normal aging, the sign of years of wear that results in gradations of color and shading on the edges of tables, on the arms of chairs, and in carvings, is often highly prized and is referred to as patina. On the other hand, less attractive signs of wear are glass rings, spots of ink, grease stains, and burns. These detract from the appearance of the piece and should be removed wherever possible.

With the exception of burns, which can be removed only by sanding (often at the expense of the aged appearance of the wood), most stains can be removed by judicious application of bleaches or acids. Inkstains can usually be removed by bleaching with laundry bleach or oxalic acid, but some kinds of ink will respond only to bases such as household ammonia or baking soda. Inkstains that don't respond to the acids will frequently bleach out with bases. Baking soda is the weakest of the basic bleaches and will not affect the color of the wood, so try it first. Mix a little into a paste, apply it to the spot, and wash it off after it has dried. If this doesn't work, try ammonia, applying it with a brush and being careful to get as little as possible on the wood surrounding the stain. Work slowly, covering the spot and rinsing it off with water almost immediately to avoid darkening the wood by overexposure to ammonia. Finally neutralize the ammonia with white vinegar.

Grease stains from both animal or vegetable fat will come out when a piece is stripped and washed with TSP. Stubborn spots that remain will usually respond to solvents such as those found in commercial spot removers of the type sold in dry-cleaning stores. Alternatively, acetone can also be used with good results. Apply directly to the spot with a small brush, let it sit for a few minutes, and blot it up with a paper towel or soft rag. Repeat until all traces of the stain are gone. But if oil has penetrated deeply it is nearly impossible to remove. However, applying an oil finish (see p. 159) may blend it in.

While it is possible to remove spots selectively, most of the spot removers will also affect the color of the wood. The result is frequently a stain replaced by a light or dark spot. When this happens, you can try to alter the color of the resulting spot so that it matches the rest of the piece. For example, light spots left from removing a stain with bleach can be darkened by applying stain. But here, too, matching the color of the surrounding wood to a spot is a painstaking process. The easiest way out is simply to treat the entire surface with bleach after removing the stain. This will make it a uniform color, and wood stains can be used to match it with the rest of the piece.

Chemically Aging Wood

THE PATINA QUESTION

"Patina" is a word that gets thrown around a lot by antique collectors, refinishers, and dealers. The identification and preservation of patina has grown into a kind of antiquers' mystique. Patina is very real and its formation is no mystery. It is simply the effect of aging and use on a piece of wood, the combined effects of the wood's drying out and losing its natural oils, changing chemically as a result of exposure to air and sunlight and moisture, and long years of being handled, dirtied, rubbed, and cleaned.

The result is a rich surface texture that is unique to each piece of wood. It is delicate, does not penetrate much below the surface of the wood, and can easily be destroyed by harsh sanding. The preservation of patina on old furniture has become an obsession to many workers. And yet, any finishing operation will have some effect on it simply because the refinisher is working on the wood, using chemicals to remove old finishes (and much of what looks like patina is frequently the effect of aging on the old finish), sanding and smoothing, and using other chemicals to apply a new finish.

The object of refinishing old furniture should, of course, be to alter the condition of the wood as little as possible. Overly arduous workmanship can produce a piece that looks more like a modern reproduction than a restored antique.

Because the patina reflects the environment and use of a particular piece of wood and is unique to it, patina can be faked but never really duplicated. Where the effect of aging is painfully obvious is when a piece of furniture has been repaired with a new piece of wood. It is virtually impossible to match new and old wood, even when there is only a 10-year difference between the pieces. And matching a piece of wood on a 150-year-old table is even more difficult. As a result, skilled furniture restorers will go to great lengths to obtain wood of the same age as the piece of furniture to be repaired. They may pirate wood from other, less valuable furniture of the same age or remove it from buildings built at the same time as the furniture.

Some workers will attempt to stain a new piece of wood to match an old one, but unfortunately new and old wood will react to stains in very different ways. Getting a perfect match is close enough to being impossible to make it a frustrating, time-consuming task that will produce dubious results.

The changes that occur with age are more pronounced with softwoods than hardwoods. This is particularly obvious with pine. The rich honey color of old pine cannot be duplicated with stain or finishing techniques on new pine. Because pine was readily available and easily worked, it was frequently used to make utilitarian early-American furniture. In many cases these pieces were given a coat of paint or simply oiled—appearance was not a major consideration, only function. Yet with age, the wood has become highly prized for its soft, warm coloration.

New pine, such as is found in unfinished furniture or is used for shelves, cannot be finished to look like old pine. In the new wood, there is high contrast between the different grain markings. These bands of grain absorb stain at different rates, often accentuating the differences rather than concealing them. Using pine stains and "antique" finishes will not conceal the fact that the wood is new, but will produce an attractive piece.

There are, however, chemical means of altering the wood so that the grain markings stand out less. And while this is by no means a way of creating the appearance or patina of old pine, it does make it possible for the finisher to create finished pine furniture, shelves, or whatever that has a mellow, even appearance and is much more pleasing to the eye than untreated pine.

ACID "AGING"

Unless you are in the business of faking antiques, chemical aging is simply a means of evening out grain markings so the wood surface will accept stain more uniformly and readily. The effect is most pronounced on the softwoods—it will even out pine and lend character to bland, uninteresting woods like birch and beech—but it can also be used on hardwoods like oak or cherry to open the grain and produce a mellower coloration.

What we are talking about here should not be thought of as a way of faking the appearance of aged wood. That is a different subject in which forgers of antiques have become very adept, using techniques like immersing in dirty water for years, burning, beating, dirtying, and generally brutalizing new reproductions until they look as if they had been used for three hundred years and spent the next hundred or so doing duty as a workbench in someone's garage. The technique of chemically aging wood is, like bleaching, simply a way of altering the appearance of wood in a manner that cannot be accomplished with stains or finishes. In some ways it mimics the effect of aging, but is no substitute. What it does do is give the finisher another means of controlling the color and appearance of the final product to create a better visual impression.

Dilute sulfuric acid can be used to even out the grain of wood. The acid removes some of the oils and resins that clog the pores of the new wood. This opens the pores in areas of dense grain so that the wood will accept stain more readily.

Before treating the wood with acid, wash it thoroughly with strong detergent. This will remove any excess oils on the surface of the wood. Then dilute 1 part of commercial-grade sulfuric acid—which can be purchased from some photographic or chemical supply houses—in 10 parts of cold water, adding the acid slowly to the water. *Never* add water to acid—it will boil up and splatter.

Be Extremely Careful: Sulfuric acid is one of the most potent acids and it can cause severe burns. Always work near a source of running water. In addition, keep a bucket full of a solution of water mixed with about a half box of bicarbonate of soda. If any acid comes in contact with the skin, flush the area immediately with the bicarb solution to neutralize the acid. Wear rubber gloves when applying acid.

Use an old nylon paint brush to thoroughly wet the surface of the wood with acid. The wood should absorb the acid almost immediately. Some woods, however, are so oily that the acid will bead up and run off like water. This, of course, is the property that prevents them from accepting stain. In such cases, add a small amount of liquid detergent to the acid solution. This will act as a wetting agent. Apply additional acid as necessary to keep the surface wet for at least five minutes. Wash the paint brush in the bicarbonate solution and rinse in clear water. Set the piece aside, in a place where people are not likely to touch the surface, for about 24 hours. Then neutralize the acid by wiping the surface with an old rag soaked with a solution of bicarbonate of soda. The surface of the wood may be oily or greasy from resins that have risen from the wood as a result of the acid treatment. This can be removed by washing the wood with a strong detergent.

Allow the piece to dry thoroughly—at least a couple of days. When it is completely dry, treat it as unfinished wood. Sand out any roughness caused by water raising the grain, and proceed with finishing. The effect of the acid will not be obvious until a stain is applied. The wood will appear slightly darker but will not be "burned" by the acid. There is, in fact, no way with such dilute acid to turn a piece of wood into a charred ruin. What the acid does is remove water and resin from the wood. This effect is very nearly the same as what takes place very slowly as wood ages. The wood will now accept stain with much less difference between the streaks of dense and open-grained wood.

5

Sanding and Smoothing

Stripping and bleaching should have removed all traces of earlier finishes and left the surface of the wood clean and ready to accept a new finish. Chemical aging of new or bleached wood will have left a surface with a color that is compatible with stains and that will readily accept stains and fillers.

The next step, and one that is every bit as critical, is to provide a surface of maximum smoothness. A satiny smooth final finish cannot be achieved over a rough surface, no matter how carefully it is applied. To sand a surface to the proper smoothness, the correct abrasives must be used and simple but extremely important procedures must be followed. Careless sanding can do more harm than good, leaving scratches that will be magnified by the final finish coats.

In sanding wood, the objective is to reach the maximum smoothness with the least possible sanding. This is not as critical with new wood, where as much of the wood as necessary can be sanded away without affecting the appearance; it is very important with old wood, where excessive sanding will remove the aged surface layer. Fortunately, all furniture was sanded smooth before the original finish was applied, so if you are careful not to mar or roughen the wood unnecessarily while removing the old finish, you can restore the surface to the proper smoothness with little effort and with minimal effect on the aged outer layer of the wood.

About Sandpaper

SELECTING THE PROPER ABRASIVE

Although it is commonly called sandpaper, the abrasives used are natural mineral and man-made materials, not sand. The term dates back to a time when sand glued to paper was used. Earlier furniture makers smoothed wood by rubbing the surface with fine sand. "Paper" is also often a misnomer; cloth and waterproof fiber backings are used on some of the more expensive, special purpose "sandpapers."

Four types of abrasives are commonly used:

Flint. This is the tan, sandy-colored abrasive that most people think of as sandpaper. It is a white quartz, a natural abrasive that is low in cost but does not have very sharp cutting edges and dulls rapidly in use. These are the cheapest types of sandpaper to buy but may actually turn out to be among the more expensive to use, because they wear out quickly and do not do as effective a job as other kinds. They should not be used in cabinetmaking and refinishing, except for sanding surfaces that quickly clog the paper, necessitating throwing it away before a more expensive abrasive would be worn out.

Garnet. Garnet is one of the hardest natural abrasives; it is sharp and has a long cutting life. Papers coated with this reddish tan mineral (which is also a semiprecious stone used in jewelry) were long preferred by commercial finishers because they outlasted flint paper many times over. However, garnet papers are less used now that superior man-made abrasives are available.

Aluminum Oxide. Made by fusing bauxite in an electric furnace at extremely high temperatures, this reddish brown abrasive is even sharper and harder than garnet and has pretty much supplanted that material in sandpaper. It costs only slightly more than garnet paper but wears better and cuts faster. It is the best all-around abrasive for wood-finishing work and can also be used on metal, plastics, and other materials.

Silicon Carbide. This is another man-made abrasive, which approaches the diamond in hardness but has the drawback of being brittle and easily fractured. It is used on very coarse-grained papers for sanding paint off floors; in fine wood finishing it is used only in very fine grades to rub down finishes between coats. The abrasive particles are black.

Sandpaper Grades and Grits

Sandpaper is made in a wide range of grit sizes, the coarser abrasives used for rougher work and the finest for final smoothing. The grains of abrasive are sorted according to the size of a mesh through which they will fall, and the mesh numbers are marked on the back of the paper. Grit sizes commonly range from 12 to 600, the designations indicating the number of holes per square inch of mesh. In other words, the smaller the number, the coarser the abrasive.

For general use, most manufacturers also mark the back of the papers with grade designations that vary from manufacturer to manufacturer, but they are a reasonable approximation that is adequate for most users.

Abrasive papers are available in either open-coat or closed-coat forms. In the open-coat type the grains of abrasive occupy only 50 to 70 percent of the area of the paper. The

ABRASIVE PAPER GRADES AND THEIR USES

Grade	Grit Number	Principal Uses
Very Coarse	12 to 30	Rarely used in wood finishing, except to smooth extremely rough wood and as first sanding of floors
Coarse	36 to 50	Heavy sanding to smooth very rough wood; reducing the thickness of wood; removing coats of paint or finish
Medium	60 to 100	Routine sanding of stripped or planed raw wood to remove scratches and imperfections
Fine	120 to 150	Final smoothing of raw wood that is to be painted
Very fine	180 to 220	Final smoothing of raw wood; sanding sealer coat and after staining
Extra fine	240 to 320	Light sanding between finish coats
Super Fine	400 to 600	Polishing of finish coats before rubbing

Note: Gradings apply to aluminum oxide, silicon carbide, and garnet papers. They express approximate ranges: grade designations and grit sizes vary from manufacturer to manufacturer. Flint papers are frequently not marked with grit number and may sometimes carry an old designation system; however, they are of little importance in finishing, having been replaced by superior abrasives.

grains, therefore, are quite far apart, causing the paper to cut more slowly but making it more resistant to clogging with particles of finish or sawdust. The closed-coat type cuts faster and more evenly but will clog more quickly. Except in cases where sappy soft wood is being sanded or coats of old paint or varnish are being sanded off, use closed-coat paper. Because of the separation of the abrasive particles on open-coat paper, the sanding is less even and more grades have to be used to achieve the required smoothness.

Most abrasives used in woodworking and finishing have either paper or cloth backings. Both are supplied in several different weights depending on the amount of rough treatment to which they are expected to be exposed. Generally, the coarser grits are supplied with heavier backings, but most papers are available in a couple of weights. The backing should be flexible enough to bend during use without cracking. Since paper-backed abrasives are less expensive, they are the best starting point. If paper backing cracks, switch to cloth.

The finer abrasives are more frequently used with cloth backings to provide maximum flexibility in use. Some cloth backings on the fine-grade papers are waterproof so that they can be used for wet sanding, a finish technique that gives the maximum smoothness.

Sanding

Sanding wears away imperfections and irregularities in the surface of the wood or finish by making thousands of tiny scratches on the surface. The coarser the grit of the paper, the bigger the scratches. Each successively finer grade of sandpaper obliterates the scratches made by the previous grade. The cardinal rule of sanding is always to start with the finest possible grade of paper that will do the job. The effect of a too coarse paper will be to roughen the surface rather than smooth it. This just makes more work (more grades of paper have to be used before the desired smoothness is obtained) and means that more material has to be removed from the surface.

Start sanding with the finest grade that will not clog immediately. A Medium paper with a grit size of about 80 is a good first choice, although softwoods will require starting with a coarser paper than hardwoods because they tend to produce larger particles during sanding and clog paper more rapidly. Use successively finer grades until the wood is as smooth as it will get with a sandpaper of about 200 grit (Very Fine). At this point the wood can be stained and filled before proceeding to Extra Fine and applying a finish.

Before sanding, carefully inspect for nails, holes, and deep gouges. Nails should be sunk with a nail set so that their heads are well below the surface of the wood to avoid snagging and tearing the sandpaper. Nailholes and other holes should be filled or patched before sanding. Use a water-based wood putty and avoid plastic-resin wood dough types (see Chapter 2). The plastic varieties do not accept stain and dry out in the can. The water-types are supplied as a powder that can be mixed in the quantity needed, accept stain readily, and are less expensive. They can be purchased at hardware and paint stores.

If very large areas require filling, it is sometimes better to cut out the damaged area and replace it with a new piece of wood (see Chapter 2). With large cracks that have been caused by drying over the years and cannot be closed by clamping and regluing, it is sometimes better to leave them rather than making an obvious patch. Just round off the edges slightly, and proceed with finishing.

As you sand, inspect the surface from time to time for rough spots. At first, running the hand over the surface will usually suffice, but with finer sanding minor differences that may show up in the final finish will not be detectable to the hand. A good way to test for perfect smoothness is to rub the surface with a piece of nylon stocking held over the fingertips. The nylon will snag on rough spots. Visual inspection can also be surprisingly accurate. Look across the surface, toward a source of light, with the eye held just above the surface. Ridges, rough spots, and other irregularities will be clearly visible.

To attain the smoothest possible surface, especially with softwoods, wet the surface with water and let it dry before sanding with the finest grade of sandpaper. This causes the tiny fibers at the surface of the wood to rise so that they can be sanded off. If they are not sanded off at this point, they will swell when the first coat of sealer is applied, producing a roughened surface. Since softwoods like pine tend to be more fibrous than hardwoods, the effect is more pronounced.

Some finishers recommend stiffening the fibers with shellac, claiming that this allows them to get an even smoother finish. They wet the fibers, let them dry, and then cover the surface with a thin coat of shellac. The shellac should be very dilute (1 part shellac to 5 parts alcohol) and brushed on in the thinnest possible layer. When the shellac is thoroughly dry, proceed with sanding. The idea is that the shellac will stiffen the fibers so that they are more closely cut by the sandpaper.

After sanding, the wood must be completely freed of all sanding dust, loose abrasive from sandpaper, or other dirt. Any residue left on the wood when finishes are applied can interfere with staining, filling, and finishing. Carelessness at this point can ruin a good finish. Clean the surface by wiping with old rags or going over it with a vacuum cleaner. A vacuum cleaner is especially handy to remove dust from cracks or from crevices in carvings and turnings. Then wipe the surface with a clean cloth and finally wipe it down with either a lint-free rag dampened with turpentine or a tack rag (see p. 15).

Hand Sanding

The key to successful hand sanding is *always sand with the grain*. This cannot be overstressed. Sanding across the grain will tear the fibers of the wood, leaving a surface that will be rough under the finish even if the finest grades of sandpaper were used. Always keep a firm, steady pressure on the paper. Bearing down as hard as you can will not get the job done any faster: instead, you run the risk of grinding particles of abrasive into the surface of the wood, possibly making deep scratches that will have to be sanded out later.

The only way to be certain that the pressure is even is to use a sanding block. These range from commercial sandpaper holders made from either metal or plastic and sold in paint and hardware stores to simple homemade devices cut from blocks of scrap wood. Many workers simply use a scrap of wood about 4 by 6 inches in size. Wrap the sandpaper around the block (a piece of two-by-four works nicely) and go to work. While this works quite nicely, a block with a padded surface works even better. That way particles of abrasive that come loose from the sandpaper will not be ground into the wood. A better sanding block can be made by gluing a piece of felt or carpet padding to the wooden surface. Blackboard erasers also work quite well.

SANDING FLAT SURFACES

A sanding block will enable you to keep an even, controlled pressure on the sandpaper. The result will be a surface that is not only smooth but flat. When hand-sanding flat surfaces, always use a sanding block. Take short strokes and work your way back and forth across the surface, sanding with the grain. The reason for short strokes is that the further you extend your arm in a stroke, the lighter the pressure becomes. When sanding out to an edge, do not let the block extend past the edge before reversing the stroke. This will prevent the block from rocking on the edge and gradually rounding it off. A small block—4 by 6 inches or so—is fine for small surfaces, but big jobs like tabletops require a bigger block— up to the size of half a sheet of sandpaper.

SANDING EDGES

Always use a sanding block on edges. Be careful to hold it evenly on the surface to prevent making a round edge in place of a square one. With both soft and hard woods, use the finest grade of sandpaper possible. This is particularly true if any of the edges present endgrain (they usually do). Endgrain is difficult to sand smooth—particles of wood tend to break out of the grain, leaving a rough edge no matter how long you sand. The only way to get a perfectly smooth endgrain surface is to sand with the finest grades of sandpaper and use very little pressure at the end. Properly done, the edge can be as smooth as glass.

If the edges are sharp when you have finished an edge, round them off ever so slightly with a couple of strokes with very fine sandpaper. This will make the edge less prone to breaking and will allow the finish to adhere more strongly to the edge. On a very sharp edge the finish will be very thin and will wear off very quickly in use.

SANDING RUNGS, SPOKES, AND MARQUETRY

Turned rungs and spokes and decorative veneer marquetry are exceptions to the rule of always sanding with the grain. In these cases, there is no way to avoid sanding against the grain. But when sanding against the grain is necessary, a passable job can be achieved by using the finest possible grades of sandpaper with light pressure to avoid tearing the wood fibers as much as possible.

Sanding curved surfaces like chair legs and rungs requires some ingenuity. Straight, round sections that have not been turned in a pattern of bulges and moldings are fairly easy: wrap the sandpaper around the rung and run it back and forth with the hand. Intricate turnings are another story. A good trick is to tear Very Fine cloth-backed sandpaper into strips between ½ and 1 inch wide. These can be pulled back and forth through the grooves with a sawing motion. Bulges and knobs have to be sanded by rubbing with paper that has been wrapped around them. Unless great care is exercised they will become flattened. Try to move the sandpaper in a circular pattern and be careful not to sand too long in one place.

Since the grain on individual pieces of veneer marquetry will run in any number of different directions, sanding with the grain is impossible. Unless you are looking for a convenient way to go mad, do not try to sand the individual pieces. Disregard the grain altogether. Use Very Fine sandpaper and sand in a direction perpendicular to the angle from which it will usually be viewed. In other words, pretend it has grain in one direction and pick the most natural direction for the grain. The best idea is to sand according to the grain of the base wood. Always use a sanding block and keep pressure light and as even as possible. Veneers can be very thin and a piece can be ruined if they are sanded too deep.

Machine Sanding

Sanding machines are indispensable to the professional finisher and can save the amateur refinisher a great deal of time. Two types of sanders have a place in finishing: orbital "finishing" sanders and belt sanders. Another type, disk sanders, make circular scratches in the wood and should never be used. They are meant for metal.

FINISHING SANDERS

These are by far the most useful sanding machines for both the professional and the amateur woodworker. They come in many sizes and price ranges, but all are basically similar. Finishing sanders are small, hand-held machines that accept flat sheets of sandpaper, which are clamped to a padded plate. The motor drives the plate with either an orbital or a reciprocating action (although some have a switch that allows the user to select either motion). The particles of abrasive on the sandpaper move back and forth in a straight line with the reciprocating type. This results in a very smooth final finish, but the sander must always be moved in the direction of the grain and it will not cut quite as fast as the orbital type. In an orbital sander, the abrasive grains transcribe small circles. As a result, the individual particles of abrasive will cut across the grain part of the time. However, the circles are so small that perceptible scratching or roughening of the surface does not occur. In theory, it is not possible to achieve the smoothness possible with a reciprocating sander using an orbital type, but with very fine sandpaper grits the difference between the two is negligible. Fussy workers finish the job with a light hand-sanding with the finest grit.

Because orbital sanders do not have to be moved in the direction of the grain and cut faster than the reciprocating types, they are more popular. The more expensive professional models operate at 10,000 to 12,000 strokes per minute; the type designed for home craftsmen at about 4,000. Both work well, although the professional ones obviously work faster. And last longer.

While finishing sanders can do the job much faster than hand sanding, they do not cut so fast that there is a risk of ruining the job by cutting too deeply. They may be used on any flat surface and, because the uniformity of their strokes is much greater than can be achieved with hand sanding, they generally do a flatter, more even job.

The only important thing to remember when using a finishing sander is not to try to force it by bearing down. They work most effectively when the only pressure on them is their own weight (and the weight of your hand). Additional pressure, caused by forcing the sander against the work surface, will slow down the motor and this will not only shorten its life, it will also cause it to cut more slowly. Let the sander do the sanding and simply guide it slowly over the work surface. Move it in a pattern that exposes all parts of the surface to an equal amount of sanding. Never let a power sander sit in one place while running—you'll dig a hole that you'll only have to sand out later, and you may damage the wood.

BELT SANDERS

Belt sanders are more specialized and less versatile than finishing sanders. They do have a place in wood finishing but it is limited to large flat surfaces and heavy cutting. Final sanding can never be accomplished with a belt sander; hand sanding or a finishing sander must be used.

Unlike finishing sanders, which have a moving plate that carries sheets of sandpaper, belt sanders have two rotating drums that move a continuous 2-to-4-inch-wide belt. Since the belts travel very fast, these are the most difficult portable sanders to use. They cut extremely rapidly and if left in place for a second they will bite deeply into the wood.

However, it is their speed of cutting that makes them useful. They are invaluable on big jobs or where wood is very rough and requires considerable coarse sanding. They are about the only thing that makes refinishing wood paneling or wainscoting practical. In addition, they can smooth a piece of old, unplaned rough-cut lumber in minutes and can cut minor warps off an old tabletop in seconds.

They are also both more expensive to buy and more expensive to operate than finishing sanders. Where finishing sanders simply use pieces of the same kinds and grits of sandpaper as used for hand sanding, belt sanders require special sanding belts. These belts are much more expensive than sheet sandpaper and are sometimes difficult to find in the finer grades.

When using a belt sander, always start the machine before you bring it in contact with the wood. If you start it in place it will cut a gouge before you have time to move it. Set the running machine onto the wood gently and move it forward as you put it down. Keep the sander moving evenly the entire time it is in contact with the wood and lift it off the surface before turning it off. Avoid letting the end of the sander extend more than ⅓ of its length beyond an edge, and be careful that the weight of the machine does not cause it to bear down heavily on an edge, rounding it off.

Steel Wool

Steel wool is flat, shredded steel that is sold in pads of varying fineness. It has several important uses in wood finishing, including wiping up finish that has been softened by remover, and smoothing wood.

Its action in wood smoothing is neither as efficient as abrasive paper nor as easy to control. However, it is a very useful material for final smoothing, one that is ignored by many finishers. While sandpaper will level off irregularities in the wood, steel wool will leave a polished surface without cutting down high spots. For this reason it is useful on old pieces where flaws and imperfections left by the maker are desirable but a smooth surface is required to apply a new finish. It is also useful for smoothing crevices and grooves in turnings, such as table and chair legs, where sandpaper is difficult to use. Another use is to roughen finishes slightly between coats to provide a better gripping surface for subsequent applications of finish.

Steel wool is supplied in pads and is usually sold in packages of sixteen. It is manufactured in seven grades; the opposite of sandpaper, the larger the number, the coarser the steel wool.

The grades of steel wool are:

3, 2, and 1. The coarsest grades available. In refinishing, their only use is cleaning up very heavy finish-remover sludge.

0. For final clean-up after stripping but before bleaching and sanding. It is used to remove final traces of remover and softened finish.

00 and 000. For smoothing endgrain and edges, as a replacement for sandpaper in places where sandpaper cannot be easily used, for removing rough spots between finish coats, and for roughening finish coats to give "tooth" for the next coat.

0000. The finest grade available. It is used to smooth the final finish coats before rubbing and for cleaning finishes with wax (which would obviously clog sandpaper even if grades fine enough were available).

Steel wool differs from sandpaper in that it works best with greater pressure. Hold the pad firmly in the hand and bear down hard on the surfaces. With bare wood, bear down as hard as you can. Between finish coats, apply light pressure—but be careful; the finish can be damaged. Also, when using steel wool over a finish, don't linger in one place; you will be building up frictional heat that can damage a finish.

The shredded fibers of metal that make up steel wool can be sharp and may penetrate the skin, so it is a good idea to wear gloves when working with it. Also, tiny fragments of the fibers will break off during use. Avoid working in a windy spot where they could be blown into the eyes.

The life of a steel-wool pad can be prolonged by knocking the dust out of the pad from time to time during use. When a pad seems to have lost its ability to cut, turn it inside out, exposing new fibers to the cutting surface.

6

Staining, Sealing, and Filling

Staining, sealing, and filling the pores of the wood are the final steps before applying a finish. They are done to highlight the natural grain, protect the wood, and provide an absolutely smooth surface for the finish coats.

Contrary to the belief of many beginners, staining is not usually done in the interest of fakery. Rather, it is a legitimate technique for enhancing the texture and natural grain of the wood. Proper staining hides nothing—instead it allows the wood to express itself in a more pleasing manner. Nor is it obtrusive—most fine old pieces of antique furniture were stained and, as a result, very few people would be able to identify some of the more common furniture woods if they were finished without staining. For instance, mahogany is not red. It is a light brown wood that early workers stained red to bring out its grain, establishing a style that has continued to the present.

This is not to say that stains cannot be used to make things look like what they aren't. In woods like walnut, they can be used to smooth out sap streaks to produce an even, uniform color. Or they can be used to conceal imperfections, mask inferior pieces of wood, or match the color of adjacent pieces of wood. While these involve altering the "natural" color of the wood, they allow the finisher to create a piece of furni

107

ture with even, uniform coloration, more attractive grain, and better overall appearance.

Besides, with or without staining, the only "natural" finish is bare wood. Even in these times when natural is held at a high premium, there are few people who would find an unfinished Chippendale chair attractive. The fact is that putting any finish—be it oil, varnish, or just wax—on to wood changes its characteristics and alters its color. Not as much as stain, perhaps, but enough so that it could never be taken for bare wood.

Stain, of course, can be used in full-out fakery. Skilled use of stains has enabled craftsmen to turn bland structural woods like poplar, birch, or beech into just about every fine cabinet wood imaginable. Many pieces of modern, low-cost, factory-made furniture sold as cherry or walnut are nothing more than white secondary woods and maybe some plywood with a thin layer of real veneer, cleverly stained to create the appearance of fine wood.

From time to time, the refinisher may remove the old coats of finish from a cherry table, only to find it is really pine. In this case, particularly if it is grandmother's dining-room table, turning it back into cherry may save some family relationships. Otherwise, there is absolutely nothing wrong with old pine. And even pine can be enhanced by staining.

Of course every wood need not be stained. Old pine that has been darkened and mellowed by age is beautiful just the way it is. Maple is so dense that it barely accepts stain and, short of painting it, it will always look like maple. There is really nothing wrong with unstained wood. But there is also nothing wrong *with* staining.

Staining, however, should be approached with care. While there is nothing difficult about applying a stain to a wood, anything done at this stage will show through the final finish coats. The object should be to give the wood a pleasing color, blend out imperfections, and bring up the grain and figure of the wood. Overstaining can be a disaster. The result will be a muddy, streaky finish that might as well have been paint for all the grain that shows through. The key to staining: know when to stop.

Like staining, filling can be another way of enhancing the grain of wood. Fillers are used to fill the open pores of the wood, providing an absolutely smooth surface for the finish that could never be fully realized with sandpaper. No matter how much you sand, the pores are always there. Pigments incorporated into the filler will cause the grain pattern to stand out in a way that no stain can achieve. Because oak is a very open-grained wood, dark-colored fillers are usually used to fill the pores, producing the familiar dark bands found on most finished oak furniture. Without this use of fillers, oak would be a uniform, sandy color.

Both the filler and the stain are covered with a coat of sealer, usually shellac, that is allowed to dry before applying further coats of finish. This is to anchor them in place and prevent pigments and dyes from dissolving in the finish, resulting in a muddy appearance rather than the deep transparency found in fine finishes.

Staining

ABOUT STAINS

Staining is simply the method of applying color to the outer layers of wood. Stains can be either dyes that penetrate the wood or ground pigments like those used in paints. They are either dissolved in solvents or suspended in a liquid medium such as oil.

There are five basic types of stains:

Water-Soluble Stains. These are used by professional furniture makers but require some skill to apply. They are bought as powders from large paint-supply stores and can sometimes be difficult to find. The reason for their popularity among professional finishers is that they produce brilliant, clear colors that will not fade when exposed to sunlight. The colors are produced by water-soluble aniline dyes. Stains are prepared by simply mixing the powdered dye with water that has been heated to just below the boiling point. The powder is poured into the water in the ratio of 1 ounce to 1 quart. When the stains have cooled they may be mixed with others to produce the desired shade for staining. To produce weaker shades they may be diluted.

While they have the advantage of producing low-cost, colorfast stains that are compatible under all finishes, water stains have some disadvantages. Their main drawback is that they raise the grain of the wood, necessitating sanding after application. This, of course, involves sanding off some of the stain that you've just put on and may mean recoating before a dark enough tone is reached. To some extent, wetting the wood, letting it dry, and sanding before the stain is applied will minimize sanding afterward, but it makes staining a lengthy process. And under any circumstances, water-based stains are the most time-consuming to use: they need at least 12 hours to dry before they can be recoated or finish coats can be applied.

They can be applied by wiping, brushing, or spraying. The surface is moistened with water, the stain applied and then blended in by wiping with a cloth. Use long even strokes that pick up the excess stain and work the remainder into the wood.

Pigment-Oil Wiping Stains. Unlike the previous stains, which get their color from a soluble dye, these are based on ground pigments, such as those used in paints, that are suspended in a carrier of oil. These are by far the most widely used and the best bet for the home finisher. They produce rich colors, are easily applied, and do not raise the grain. These are the stains that are most commonly sold in little cans in paint and hardware stores. In reality they are nothing more than a thin paint that has been formulated to dry slowly (about 12 hours), although newer, fast-drying (30 minutes) types are available.

Oil wiping stains allow the worker ample time to even out color before they dry, and there is little danger of overlaps showing as darker areas. They are usually applied by wiping with a cloth, but brush or spray can also be used. Once applied to the wood, they are allowed to sit until the surface begins to look dull; then the excess is wiped off with a clean cloth.

Penetrating Oil Stains. These are oil stains formulated with dyes that are soluble in oil. They are similar to water stains in that they are transparent, although the colors are not as lightfast as those used in water stains. Oil stains may bleed into the finish coats unless they are properly sealed.

On the plus side, penetrating oil stains are fairly easy to apply and do not raise the grain of the wood. They dry in 2 to 4 hours, permitting work to proceed fairly soon afterward. They are recommended for use on coarse, open-grain woods that might become clogged by pigment stains. Some commercially formulated oil stains contain both pigments and dyes.

Non-Grain-Raising Stains. Like water stains, these produce clear, lightfast colors but, unlike water stains, they do not raise the grain. The reason is that they are dyes dissolved in solvents that do not cause the fibers of the wood to swell and lift.

They are, however, difficult to use. They dry almost instantly and cannot be reworked without leaving dark areas. While some manufacturers suggest brush application, skill is required and results are often dubious. Spraying is about the only effective means of applying these stains evenly.

Because of the solvents used, they are more expensive than their water-based counterparts. They are available in a wide range of readily mixed colors.

Alcohol-Soluble Stains. These stains, which are also called spirit stains, are the fastest-drying of all and are, consequently, the most difficult to use. They are made from powdered dyes that are dissolved in methyl alcohol and dry sufficiently to be recoated in 5 to 10 minutes. As a result they are rarely used as a basic wood stain, even by professionals. Instead they are used for quick final touch-ups. They fade seriously when exposed to sunlight.

Getting the Right Color

While the selection of a stain that can be applied and controlled to give an even coloration to the wood is certainly important, the critical step with staining is the selection of the proper color. This, unfortunately, is a subjective process and one that can be very confusing to the beginner. A trip to the paint or hardware store will provide little solace. The shopper is confronted with rows of little cans of stain with pretentious names and accompanying color samples that are supposed to show the final color of the stain on the wood for which it is intended. One manufacturer's light oak may be the same color as another's fruitwood. And when they are put on the wood, the resulting color may show little or no resemblance to the sample on a color chart. Just because your project is made from mahogany does not mean that it will take stain the same way as the manufacturer's samples. Unless two pieces of wood were cut from the same tree and had the same history, they will neither look the same nor stain in the same manner.

The easiest way out of this confusing situation is to ignore it. Stains are simply pigments and dyes suspended or dissolved in various carriers. There is nothing mysterious about them at all. Nor is there any necessity to use one fancy formulation on one kind of wood and not on another. All that stain makers have done is to combine commonplace shades of red, blue, yellow, and black in ways that they think bring out the best of particular woods. By forgetting about the fancy names and the fact that the can says one stain should be used for oak and another for pine, selecting the proper color becomes a relatively easy process.

BLENDING COMMERCIAL STAINS

Since stains are nothing more than mixtures of colors, they can be blended by the user to achieve any shade desired. The objective of staining is to highlight and accentuate the color of the wood—and most furniture woods do not come in very many colors. The majority of woods used by furniture makers are various shades of brown ranging from the dark tones of walnut to the pale sandy color of white oak. Some, like cherry and mahogany, have a reddish cast and others, like maple or pine, an orange or yellow cast.

By buying a small assortment of different stains, the refinisher can quickly tailor the stain to the exact shade that is required. The following four stains can be used or blended together to produce most of the shades that a wood finisher will ever require:

Walnut—a good rich brown
Maple—a light yellow-orange
Red Mahogany—brown with strong red overtones
Light oak or fruitwood—a warm tan color

Achieving the proper color will take a little experimentation. Use a scrap of wood of the same kind as you intend to stain or, better yet, an unexposed part of the furniture itself. Pick the stain that you think is closest to the color you want and try a small area right from the can. If you think it needs more red, add mahogany; yellow, add maple; and so on. When mixing stains, use a teaspoon or other small measure and combine the stains in a small can or jar. After arriving at the right color, write the formula on the inside of the piece that you intend to stain. That way, if any repairs have to be made at a later date, you will be able to match the stain precisely. The best way to record stain formulas is in terms of parts of each component. For example, a good stain for cherry or pine is 1 part walnut and 1 part red mahogany.

This process obviously requires that you have some concept of what color you want for a particular piece of wood. With experience, it becomes possible to look at wood and know that adding red or deepening the brown tones will make an attractive stain job. The best way to gain this feeling is to obtain a number of pieces of various cabinet woods and experiment with blending stains and finding those combinations that are most appealing. But remember: staining should bring out the attractive features of the grain and coloration without hiding the natural beauty of the wood.

Experienced stainers frequently tint stains by adding pigments directly. These colors are available in tubes from paint stores and are referred to as tinting colors. Artist's colors, which are less concentrated, may be used if tinting colors cannot be obtained. An assortment of these will allow an added dimension in altering the basic color of commercial stains. The colors that a wood finisher will need are reds, yellows, blues, browns, and black. The following colors provide an adequate range for use on wood.

Absolutely essential:
  Chinese Red
  Chrome Yellow Light (pure yellow)
  Chrome Yellow Medium or Dark (orange tint)
  Vandyke Brown (has a very slight grayish cast)

Optional:
  Burnt Sienna (light reddish brown)
  Raw Sienna (light yellowish brown)
  Burnt Umber (dark brown)
  Raw Umber (dark brown with a slight reddish cast)
  Cobalt Blue (blue)
  Ultramarine Blue (blue with a reddish cast)
  Drop Black (pure dead black)

To tint stains with these colors, squeeze the tube back and forth to mix the pigment with the oil within the tube, squeeze a small amount into the stain, blend well, and test the result on the wood. Before using the stain, strain it through a piece of nylon stocking to remove any tiny lumps.

Work with small quantities until you are satisfied with the color, then mix a larger batch for use. To determine what the stain will look like when it is covered with sealer and finish, put a light coat of shellac over the test area. Most stains look darker when covered with finish. Another way to visualize the effect of finish on a stain is to apply a coat of white shellac on a piece of window glass. Setting the glass on a stained surface has an effect similar to the final finished appearance.

MIXING STAINS

For most work, stains are perfectly adequate as they come out of the can. The only problem is selecting the color that you want. To match a stain, blending commercial stains and adding pigments is perfectly adequate. Yet some finishers prefer to mix their own stains from scratch. Oil stains can be made relatively easily.

To make oil stains, simply mix tinting colors into a mixture of 1 part boiled linseed oil and 2 parts thinner. Start off by squeezing equal-sized dabs of pigment from the tubes into a small container filled with thinner. Keep track of how much of each color you use. When you have arrived at a color that you like, you can scale it up. The easiest way is to buy colors in the smallest sizes of tubes and work in ounces of pigment diluted by an equal amount of mineral spirits. If the resulting stain seems to be too strong when tested, simply add more mineral spirits. It is better to work with a slightly weak stain: you can always apply additional coats, and less intense stains are easier to control.

While most workers will prefer to experiment and develop their own formulas, a few basic stain formulas follow:

Pine: 2 parts Raw Sienna
        1 part Burnt Umber
        1 part Ultramarine Blue

Walnut: 2 parts Burnt Umber
        1 part Vandyke Brown
        1 part Burnt Sienna

Cherry: 1 part Chinese Red
        2 parts Burnt Umber
        1 part Burnt Sienna

Applying the Stain

Before staining, be sure that the surface of the wood is completely free of sanding dust and other dirt. Wipe it thoroughly with a clean, lint-free cloth, then either vacuum or blow off the surface with air from a shop compressor if you have one. (A vacuum cleaner with a hose attached to the air outlet will also work.) Finally, go over the surface with a tack rag.

Select the stain that you will use. If you are not familiar

with the intensity of the particular stain, it is a good idea to thin it down. Any commercial stain can stand thinning with an equal proportion of the appropriate thinner. That way you will reduce the chances of overstaining and, if the first application is not deep enough, a second should suffice.

All types of furniture stains can be used under varnish, wax and oil finishes, shellac, or penetrating sealers. However, oil-base stains (any stain with a label that tells you to clean your brushes in mineral spirits or turpentine) are *not* compatible with lacquer. If lacquer is applied directly over an oil-base stain it will lift and crack. Oil-base stains can be used under lacquer finishes but they must first be carefully sealed with either shellac or a compatible sealer. Both alcohol- and water-soluble stains are compatible with lacquer.

Nothing, however, is compatible with silicone-based furniture waxes. If you apply stain and it beads up, the piece was probably waxed with silicone. Silicone will penetrate through the finish and deeply into the wood—stripping and washing will not remove it. The same thing will happen to any finish applied over silicone. And nothing can be done about it. Silicone ruins furniture for any future finishing.

The best way to apply stains is by constantly wiping the surface with a rag that has been well wet with stain. Many refinishers recommend brushing stain onto the surface, letting it sit, and then wiping off the excess. But it is impossible to see how the wood is taking the stain. And overlaps can result from brush strokes unless great care is used. By wiping the area with a steady motion that covers an entire surface, the stain will be applied evenly. When the wood is stained to the desired color, wipe the area with a clean dry cloth to remove any excess.

Never attempt to stain an entire piece at one time; apply stain to as much as can be wiped completely dry in about 30 seconds. But never stain a fraction of an open surface—when you try to do the other part you will get an overlap that will show. The best method is to keep turning the piece and stain only the area that can be seen at one time. With a table, for example, turn it upside down and stain each leg, then the skirt (a complete section at a time). Turn it right-side up, and stain the top. The surfaces that show the most should always be stained last. That way they are less likely to be marred or smeared.

Because they lack large flat surfaces, chairs are about the most difficult pieces of furniture to stain. Start by laying the chair on one side and staining all surfaces of the legs and rungs that are facing you. Let the stain sit, wipe it off, and then turn the chair over and repeat on the opposite side. Next stain the back. Then, set the chair upright and stain the seat.

A good strategy for staining pieces of furniture like dressers and buffets is to start with the piece standing on one end and stain the end, legs, and underlip of the top. Try to avoid getting any stain on the surface of the top—if you do, wipe if off immediately or the stain on the top will be uneven. Do the other end, then lay the piece on its back and do the front; stand it upright, and stain the top. Leave the drawer fronts and doors (which should have been removed) until last.

The most important thing to remember about staining (and the reason that planning out the job is important) is never to stop, once you have started. Work rapidly and steadily. You are bound to overlap the stain in many places as you work. The longer the stain has set on the wood, the deeper it will have penetrated, and the more an overlap will show when the job is completed.

Woods with prominent sap streaks (pine, walnut, and cherry, in particular) present problems in staining. On fine old pieces, walnut and cherry boards were carefully selected to match evenly and pieces with sap streaks were rejected. Nobody cared enough about pine to worry about it. Later furniture makers got less choosy as the price of fine cabinet woods increased, and they began using the streaky heart-wood, disguising the streaks with stains.

After stripping a rich, brown walnut piece, the refinisher may find himself confronted with wood of the natural walnut color but with prominent streaks that are almost white. And unfortunately, the white wood contains large amounts of sap and resists penetration by stains. If an even, attractive finish is to result, these bands of lighter wood must be evened up by staining. Stain should be applied with a pad, but care must be taken not to overstain the adjacent areas. For very small areas an artist's brush may be used.

Another problem area is staining endgrain, such as is found at the ends of tabletops. Because the fibers of the wood have been cut off, endgrain is extremely absorptive and care must be taken to avoid staining it too dark. The edges of round tables are particularly bothersome: the edge of the table will progress gradually from straight grain into endgrain, and the tendency will be for it to stain darker and darker as more endgrain is exposed. Carvings are also difficult because of their exposure of endgrain and straight grain, depending upon the angle at which the wood has been cut. They are somewhat less of a problem, though, because the differential staining occurs over small areas and tends to highlight the relief of the carving.

When staining endgrain, make it as unabsorptive as possible and apply dilute stain sparingly and quickly. The smoother the endgrain, the less stain it will absorb. The reason is that smooth sanding leaves fewer exposed fibers to draw the stain into the wood. Always sand endgrain to the maximum possible smoothness—in the end you will save time, or at least, not have to live with a brown table with black edges. Saturating the endgrain with thinner before applying the stain will also reduce the ability of the wood to absorb stain.

The easiest way to deal with endgrain is to dilute the stain, apply it sparingly, and wipe it off quickly. Apply as many coats as necessary to match the flat surfaces. To stain carving, use a small brush, coat the straight-grain surfaces first, then the endgrain. Wipe with a soft cloth almost immediately.

APPLYING PIGMENT-OIL STAINS

These stains have the longest drying time of any type and for this reason are not usually used in furniture manufacturing. They are, however, the best choice for the amateur or the fine finisher because of the control the worker can exercise over the final color.

Because pigment-oil stains are a suspension of ground colors in oil, they must be thoroughly stirred before use. Unlike stains based on dyes, the pigment will settle out. These stains are wiped onto the wood, leaving the pigment in the pores. The easiest means of application is with a lint-free rag. A brush can also be used to apply stain, which is then wiped off with a rag.

Apply the stain evenly, being careful to cover entire surfaces. Immediately wipe off any stain that runs onto other surfaces. Wet the rag with additional stain as necessary. If the stain gets too dark, the excess pigment can be removed by wiping the surface with a cloth that has been wetted with paint thinner or mineral spirits.

Because of the long drying time of oil stains, putting additional stain on areas that have not absorbed enough is relatively easy and overlap marks are easy to avoid because the wiping step will blend out the stain. Let pigment-oil stains dry for 8 to 24 hours before sealing.

APPLYING PENETRATING OIL STAINS

Penetrating oil stains are similar to pigment stains except that their color comes from dissolved dyes rather than ground pigments. Penetrating oil stains are applied in the same manner as pigment-oil stains. They are always wiped onto the wood with a clean rag to produce a uniform surface. They dry more rapidly than the stains containing pigments (2 to 8 hours before applying sealer) so work must proceed more rapidly than with pigment stains, but they are also slow enough that there is little danger of their drying too soon.

APPLYING NON-GRAIN-RAISING STAINS

Because these sprayable stains dry very quickly (less than 30 minutes; some in less than 10 minutes) they are used extensively by professional finishers but are not recommended for the amateur. They should be applied with a fine spray in an even coat. Keep the spray gun moving and always work with enough light to permit judging the evenness of the color accurately. These stains should always be applied by spray because the rapid drying calls for fast, accurate work. A brush should be used only for small areas and touch-up.

The possibility of leaving visible lap marks can be reduced by thinning the stain and using more than one coat. Another trick that is sometimes used is to wet the surface with a heavy coat of solvent (alcohol or paint thinner both work) before applying the stain. The solvent will spread the stain over the surface as it dissolves in the solvent.

Warning: These stains are flammable. Be sure to have adequate ventilation, especially when spraying.

APPLYING ALCOHOL STAINS

These stains are dry almost before they reach the surface of the wood. They can be applied only by spray. They are used in special cases by professional finishers, and are not recommended for the amateur.

APPLYING WATER STAINS

The most efficient method of applying water stains is also by spraying. Use a fine spray and cover all surfaces evenly. Let it dry from 4 to 8 hours, then apply an additional coat if necessary. When the desired color is attained, let the stain dry for at least 12 hours before sealing the stain.

In the absence of spray equipment, water stains can be applied by brush. Use a clean brush and apply the stain with the work surface in a horizontal position if possible. Apply the stain with long, even brush strokes, starting at one end and working toward the other. When the surface has been covered with stain, wipe the brush on the edge of the stain container and go over the surface again, working the stain into the wood and picking up excess with the brush. Finally wipe the surface with a clean cloth. Avoid applying stain too generously; brush it on evenly, as you would paint. Putting too much stain in one area can result in a blotchy staining job.

Water stains lighten as they dry, so wait from 4 to 8 hours before deciding whether to apply additional stain. To determine what the stain will look like under a clear finish, stain a hidden test area or a similar piece of wood at the same time. When it has dried, coat part of it with shellac. If you apply a second coat of stain, apply it to the test piece as well.

Since water stains raise the grain of the wood, it is necessary to sand lightly before sealing in the stain. Use 120- to 150-grit sandpaper and be careful not to sand too much stain out of the wood. The sanding step can be minimized by wetting the wood before staining and then sanding off the "fuzz." The stain will still raise the grain but not as much.

Excessive stain absorption by endgrain can be prevented by wetting the end areas prior to staining. If they are kept wet, the wood will be much less absorptive and any stain that gets onto endgrain accidentally will be diluted and can be wiped off before it penetrates very deeply.

CLEANING YOUR HANDS

Unless you wear rubber gloves, you will probably find that your hands accept stains at least as readily as wood. Lanolin-based hand cleaners, of the type sold in hardware stores, and cold cream are both very effective. In the absence of a hand cleaner, rubbing the hands with cooking oil and then washing with liquid dish detergent does a pretty good job. Stains will also come off if the hands are washed in turpentine or mineral spirits and then with soap.

Sealing

Sealers are used to seal the pores of the wood before finishing. Many commercial finish manufacturers formulate sealers to be used with their products. These usually work quite well and are commonly nothing more than the finish itself in a thin form with the addition of chemicals to make sanding easier. As a general rule, avoid using these sealers with finishes other than the one specified. They may not be compatible with all other finishes and a whole job can be ruined.

One way to avoid that potential confusion is to use shellac as a sealer under all finishes. Shellac is compatible with every type of finish and is essential under lacquer finishes if they are to be applied over oil stains. And while it may seem to be an "old-fashioned" material, it is by far the most widely used sealer among wood finishers—and with good reason: it will seal in almost anything including pitch from knots in new pine and even roofing tar.

When shellac is used for sealing it should be thinned to what is referred to as a two-pound cut. It is usually supplied in a four-pound cut, which means that 4 pounds of dried shellac have been dissolved in 1 gallon of alcohol. A two-

pound cut means that 2 pounds of shellac have been dissolved in 1 gallon of alcohol. To reduce a four-pound cut to
two-pound cut, mix shellac and alcohol in equal parts.

For clear finishes, seal with white shellac; dark finishes can
be sealed with orange shellac. Apply the thinned shellac with
a brush or spray gun in a thin, even coat. It will seem to soak
in and disappear almost immediately. Let it dry for 1 to 2
hours (it will feel dry to the touch much sooner, but wait for
it to be absolutely dry before proceeding), and then sand
lightly with 220-grit sandpaper. If the sandpaper binds, the
surface is not yet dry enough.

There is a class of new commercial sealers called sanding
sealers. These are usually blends of shellac and either varnish
or lacquer with the addition of chemicals that make them
sand off as a fine powder rather than becoming gummy.
They are formulated for compatibility with various finishes—
read the labels carefully. The added chemicals also improve
the leveling characteristics of the sealer, causing it to flow on
evenly and fill minute depressions in the grain more effectively. The one drawback to these sealers is that the sanding
and leveling agents make the sealer slightly cloudy. This is no
problem if only one coat is to be applied, but they should
never be used to build a final finish.

Some sealers can be used both to seal and to build a final
finish, however. As a class of products they are usually called
penetrating wood sealers; while they may be used as sealers
under other finishes, their main use is as a finish that requires
no sealer. They were developed for gymnasiums and other
demanding floor finish applications but soon were taken up
in the furniture field. The first penetrating sealers to reach the
market were clear finishes with varnishlike properties and ex-
ceptional hardness that were based on tung oil.

There are now many commercial finishes based on synthetic resins such as the urethanes, vinyls, and acrylics. The
finishes are available in common wood colors (walnut, cherry, maple, etc.) as well as clear.

Some of these finishes are not compatible with many of the commonly used sealers. If you plan on using one of these finishes for the final coats, check the manufacturer's instructions carefully before you begin to work. They may require the use of a special sealer made for that finish. If they are used over a sealer with which they are incompatible, a lot of work will be lost: the finish will come off in use. Buying a special sealer can sometimes be unnecessary, though, because some manufacturers' sealers are nothing more than a dilute version of their final finishes. Remember: any finish is compatible with itself. It can simply be diluted with the appropriate thinner and applied as a sealer over stain or filler.

Filling

Fillers are used to fill the tiny pores and crevices of the grain. The proper use of filler will leave an absolutely smooth surface while enhancing the grain pattern of the wood. Since the grain of wood is composed of minute depressions that were the cells of the living tree, it is impossible to sand wood to an absolutely perfect smoothness; sanding will always open new pores. A smooth surface can be achieved only by filling these holes with another material. With closed-grain woods such as maple or pine, these pores are not much of a problem. They are so small that they are almost unnoticeable and are eventually filled by the finish coats.

The pores of medium-grained woods like apple and walnut can sometimes be filled with finish as well. As each successive finish coat is applied and rubbed down, the finish is sanded off the high areas and that in the pores remains until a smooth, level surface is built up. This can be a painstaking task and is really unnecessary work—you are applying finish (which is usually pretty expensive stuff) and then sanding most of it off.

Coarse-grained wood such as oak, chestnut, teak, and mahogany is always filled in good finishing jobs. Oak, for one, is so rough that a smooth surface cannot be obtained any other way. Occasionally, unfilled oak is sold, advertised as having the "country look." This is a manufacturer's economy move and is a waste of good wood. The surface feels rough, the grain is not attractive, and the wood is difficult to wax and keep clean.

PASTE AND LIQUID FILLERS

Commercially available fillers are sold in paste and liquid form. They are finely ground silex, a glassy mineral obtained from rock quartz, suspended in a varnishlike medium. After drying and sanding, it forms a hard foundation for finish coats.

Paste fillers are a concentrated product that is thinned down with turpentine when slow drying is desired or with naphtha if fast drying is preferred. The liquid fillers contain much less silex and are useful only on fairly closed-grain woods.

For most work, paste fillers are the best bet. They can be thinned to any consistency and are suitable for filling any type of wood. Successful filling requires diluting the filler to the proper consistency. The larger the pores to be filled, the thicker the filler required. If filler is too thin, it will pull out of the pores; but if the pores are small and thick filler is used, it will not flow into the crevices. For open-grained woods such as oak, chestnut, or ash, the filler should be the consistency of thick paint. Medium-grained woods like mahogany, walnut, and the fruitwoods require a filler the consistency of thin paint or unthinned varnish. The closer-grained woods like birch and beech require a very thin filler. Maple, fir, pine, and spruce are so close-grained that they will not accept a filler.

COMMON CABINET WOODS AND FILLERS

No Filler	Thin Filler	Medium Filler	Thick Filler
Cherry	Apple	Butternut	Ash
Fir	Beech	Mahogany	Chestnut
Hemlock	Birch	Rosewood	Elm
Magnolia	Gum	Walnut	Hickory
Maple	Pecan		Locust
Pine	Sycamore		Oak
Poplar			Teak
Spruce			

COLORING FILLERS

Fillers are always applied over wood that has already been sealed and almost always over wood that has been stained. However, fillers are usually colored. By adding color to the filler, the low spots in the grain are subtly highlighted and contrast attractively with the stained surface of the wood. A good example is oak. Oak is usually filled with a slightly darker filler that brings out the pattern of the grain. This is done so often that most people accept it as the natural coloration of the wood. In reality, oak is much less visually exciting if it is finished without colored filler.

As a general rule, fillers are usually colored so that they are slightly darker than the rest of the wood. Some manufacturers sell fillers with color already added, but this involves having a lot of filler on hand in order to blend and mix them to the desired shade. A much easier way is to buy natural filler (it dries to a light tan color) and tint by adding colors-in-oil or by mixing in small quantities of oil stain. It is a simple matter to take the stain that was used on a piece, darken it slightly, and add it to the filler. Test the filler for the correct color on the same piece of wood you used to try out the stain. If you prefer that the filler not show at all, color it with the same stain that was used on the wood.

APPLYING WOOD FILLERS

Fillers are almost always applied by brush. First thin the filler to the proper consistency and try it out on a piece of the same wood or an inconspicuous part of the furniture. Use a stiff brush and apply a generous quantity of filler to the surface of the wood. Brush it on in the direction of the grain and then immediately brush over it across the grain. Let it stand on the wood until it begins to set up. It will lose its surface gloss and become dull-looking, usually in about 20 minutes.

The filler is then packed into the crevices by wiping, and any that remains on the surface is wiped off. The best material for the initial wiping is burlap—it should be clean and cut into easily handled pieces, about a foot square. Professional wood finishers use a variety of other coarse materials including jute, sea grass, hemp fiber (which, in a pinch, can be obtained by unraveling a length of hemp rope), moss, or even wood shavings.

Make a burlap pad and wipe across the grain, using short strokes to pick up excess but packing as much filler as possible into the pores of the wood. When the surface is fairly clean, wipe in the direction of the grain with clean, lint-free rags to clean all the filler off the high points in the wood. If filler is left on the surface of the wood, the finish will have a dull, blotchy appearance. For final cleanup of filler residue, go over the surface very lightly with a cloth barely moistened with turpentine.

If the filler seems to be pulling out of the pores during the initial wiping, it has not been allowed to dry long enough. On the other hand, if it doesn't wipe clean, it was allowed to set too long. In this case, wipe with a cloth wet with turpentine. If all the filler comes out as a result, you can always fill again. In fact, the very coarse woods, oak in particular, are better if filled twice, because of the shrinkage of the large amounts of filler in the pores. Fill once, let it stand overnight, and fill again with a very thin filler solution.

Carvings are difficult to fill, and some workers don't bother because the filler may obscure some of the finer details. Carving can be filled, but thinner fillers should be used and the filler worked into the pores with a small, stiff-bristle brush of the type sold in art-supply stores for stenciling. To wipe the filler, use a picking stick made from a piece of sharpened dowel, wrap a piece of cloth around the end, and work it back and forth in the cracks.

Allow the filler to dry for at least 24 hours (48 is even better) before applying a sealer coat to the filler. Unless the filler has dried completely, the finish coats may not dry properly or graying can occur in the finish. If the filler is not protected by sealer, stains will bleed into the final finish coats. When the filler is completely dry, seal it in, sand lightly, and proceed with the final finish.

Glazing Stains

This is a specialty staining technique that shades the edges of a piece to "frame" its shape and simulate the appearance of wear. It is not a modern "faking" technique and has been used on fine furniture for years, although it is optional and in no way relates to the quality of a finish.

Glazing stains are pigmented oil stains that, like filler, are usually applied to the wood in a shade much darker than the basic stained or unstained surface. They work best on close-grained wood that will not accept filler, such as maple or birch. Since they are thinner than even the thinnest filler, they will collect in the most minute variations in the grain. This will produce a subtle darkening effect, without obscuring the wood or giving the appearance that the piece has been painted.

These stains are usually applied around the edges of tables and to carvings and moldings to create highlights and an illusion of depth. For example, years of wear will darken the top of a table or other piece of furniture near the edges because those areas are rubbed by hands more frequently and become dirtier than the center. By applying a dark stain to the edges, this mellowing effect of use is reproduced—that is, if glazing is skillfully done. Otherwise, inept or careless work can turn a fine piece of furniture into a mawkish imitation of itself.

Glazing stains are applied to the surface of the piece after it has been stained, filled, and sealed. They may be applied with brush or spray, or wiped on with a lint-free cloth. Apply the stain, which is like a thin paint, to the parts of the piece to be darkened. Let the stain sit until it has had time to set somewhat (about 30 minutes). Then carefully wipe the stain with a lint-free cloth, working from the edge in toward the center. The stain should be wiped in so that it creates a gradual, imperceptible grading from dark to light. If the blending out does not work satisfactorily, the glazing stain can be wiped off with turpentine.

Finishing can then proceed without applying an additional sealer coat, unless the piece is to be finished with lacquer. If lacquer is used, a sealer coat of two-pound-cut shellac must be applied.

Shading lacquer is sometimes used to produce similar results, although it is applied only by spray, requires skilled application, and is mainly used in production work. While it duplicates some of the effects of glazing stains, it cannot capture the effect of a skillfully applied glaze. When it is applied too heavily, it obscures the grain of the wood and produces a painted appearance. Because shading lacquer obscures the wood, it is sometimes used to make low-cost woods look like finer types.

7

Applying the Final Finish

The three most common finishes for wood furniture are varnish, shellac, and lacquer. While each has different properties that, to some extent, affect the use to which a piece of furniture can be put, the selection of the final finish is largely a matter of taste.

Most pre-Victorian furniture was originally finished with shellac, although some was painted and some simply waxed. Both varnish and lacquer became available later. For this reason shellac retains its position among wood finishes even though the more recently invented finishing materials have vastly reduced its use. Shellac finishes are unexcelled for depth and luster, particularly when they are applied by the laborious process called "French polishing." Since shellac is dissolved in alcohol, it dries very rapidly and is easy to work with. The disadvantages of shellac are that it will redissolve in alcohol and turn white when exposed to water. This makes it a less acceptable finish for surfaces that will be exposed to alcoholic beverages or wet glasses.

In terms of finish durability, varnish was a major advance over shellac. The original varnishes were made by boiling shellac and linseed oil. The shellac and the oil mix during boiling. The resulting finish is an improvement over both shellac and linseed oil. Varnish dries harder than oil and is more resistant to alcohol and water than shellac.

Today, *varnish* is a generic term for finishes made by combining a gum with an oil. Synthetic gums and a variety of oils such as tung oil are now used. This, of course, causes some confusion; there are now many different types of varnish formulated for specific purposes.

Lacquer is also a very good wood and furniture finish. It is harder than shellac and is resistant to both alcohol and water staining. The solvents in lacquer evaporate almost immediately. This is an advantage to commercial finishers because it enables them to coat a piece in a few minutes, but it requires fast, accurate work. For this reason, it is almost always applied by spray.

Varnish

SELECTING THE PROPER VARNISH

Because of the many kinds of varnish that are available, selecting the correct varnish for the job can be confusing. For most finishing applications, the toughest finish is the best, but a lot of varnishes on the market have fancy names that can lead the novice astray.

The most common misconception about varnish is that spar varnish is the toughest varnish available. And why not? It's used on boat decks and exposed to constant moisture and harsh sunlight. But on furniture, spar varnish is the worst choice. To resist the harsh environments that it is exposed to, it is formulated so that it never dries completely hard. When applied to furniture, it remains soft and has a low resistance to abrasion.

The varnishes that should be used for furniture are those that are made to produce a hard finish that is abrasion- and solvent-resistant. Some are formulated specifically for furniture finishing. These include "rubbing" and "polishing" varnishes for finishing cabinets and pianos with fine built-up finishes, in which each coat is rubbed down with pumice and oil and the final coat polished with rottenstone. Included in this category are the high-gloss finishes used on grand pianos, a finish that is an art in itself and is applied only by the most highly skilled finishers.

The rubbing and polishing varnishes are usually the best quality obtainable. The best overall varnishes for the nonprofessional finisher are the tabletop or bartop varnishes. They are very wear resistant and stand up to alcohol and water better than almost any other type of varnish. Another good choice is any of the varnishes designed for floors, particularly gymnasiums. They are every bit as good on furniture and are tough and elastic, being formulated to withstand a great deal of abrasion.

GLOSS AND SATIN VARNISH

Varnish can be varied from the highest, glassy gloss to the softest luster. On fine furniture and in the application of fine finishes, the final appearance of the finish is controlled both by the type of varnish used and by final rubbing and polishing steps (see Chapter 8). Rubbing can "knock down" a high-gloss finish to produce a soft luster or a glossy varnish can be polished to mirror smoothness.

The type of finish desired by the finisher determines the selection of the proper varnish. For most furniture work, good interior varnishes can be used to produce either satin or high-gloss finishes by rubbing and polishing. When professional finishers are applying the highest-quality finishes, however, they select rubbing and polishing varnishes. Varnishes with these designations are always of the highest quality and are usually only available through stores that supply professional finishers. What accounts for the hardness of varnishes is the ratio of resin to oil. Most furniture and interior varnishes have higher resin concentrations than exterior varnishes such as spar varnish. Polishing varnishes have the highest resin content, followed by rubbing varnishes.

For extremely glossy finishes like those applied to pianos, a number of coats of rubbing varnish precede a final coat of unthinned polishing varnish. For less glossy finishes, rubbing varnishes are sufficient.

If you wish to avoid the task of rubbing and polishing a finish, flat or satin varnishes are available. However, these should only be used for the final coat; they contain flatting agents that make the varnish slightly cloudy. With only one coat, the cloudiness is not apparent but if satin varnish is used for several coats of a finishing job, the result will be a dull finish that will obscure the grain of the wood.

The truly lazy man's varnishes are the so-called varnish stains. These are generally low-quality varnish to which stain has been added. The claim is that staining and the final finish can be applied at the same time, and while that is true, the resulting finish is usually nothing to brag about. The major problem is that the final color depends on the amount of finish. If it takes two or three coats to produce a good, smooth finish, the stain may have become so dark that it is difficult to tell what kind of wood it's been applied to.

One last factor that can affect the selection of a furniture varnish is the method of application. Most varnishes, and all the best finishes, are applied by brush. However, some varnishes have.been formulated for spraying. These are usually quicker drying and are used mainly in fast production-line work.

Applying Varnish

Varnishes are among the hardest finishes to apply. A good finish requires care both in handling the varnish itself and in applying it. Unless the work is done carefully, the results will be less than satisfactory.

Clear, gloss varnishes are ready to use as they come from the can. Stirring should be avoided. When the varnish is stirred and immediately applied, small bubbles will form on the surface and may dry without bursting. And about the only thing to do with a bubbly surface is to take the finish off and start over.

Even without stirring, bubbles are a problem. They are, however, one that can be greatly minimized by thinning the varnish prior to application. Varnish should be thinned with about 1 part of pure turpentine to about 4 parts of varnish. Thinning, of course, necessitates stirring so let the thinned varnish stand for 10 to 15 minutes before using it so that the trapped air has time to come to the surface.

Thinning accomplishes several things. Fewer air bubbles form during brushing, and those that do appear will burst and level out of their own accord. Also, the varnish brushes out more evenly, it flows better, covers faster, and dries more thoroughly and rapidly. While thinning means putting on more coats to build a finish of the proper thickness, it eliminates the danger of overly thick coats. And a number of thin coats form a harder, more even, and longer-lasting finish in any case.

There is an exception to the rule about not stirring varnishes. That is the flat or satin types, which contain flatting agents; these will settle to the bottom of the can and must be mixed into the varnish before and during application.

THE PROPER CONDITIONS FOR APPLYING VARNISH

Varnish should always be applied in a dust-free environment. While dust is a danger when applying most finishes, dust is a deadly nemesis to varnish. A freshly varnished surface is extremely sticky and will pick up airborne dust. Because varnish has a comparatively long drying time, it is more vulnerable to contamination. And because of the clarity and high gloss of varnish finishes, dust particles are very visible in the finished surface.

Before varnishing, the workroom should be vacuumed or damp-mopped to keep down the dust. Wearing a painter's cap (most paint stores have paper ones they will give you) is also a good idea to keep hair from falling onto the wet surface.

It is, of course, essential that the surfaces to be finished be absolutely free of dust and other contamination. The piece should be thoroughly wiped with a lint-free rag or a vacuum cleaner. A final wiping with a tack rag is recommended.

Varnish is also quite sensitive to temperature and humidity. For best results varnish should be applied with temperatures above 70° F. At lower temperatures, the varnish will become sticky and will not flow properly. If the varnish itself is cold (if it was stored in a cold place, for instance), warm it by placing the can in a pan of warm water.

While varnishes are manufactured to perform at normal humidities, they generally brush out more easily and dry better when the humidity is low. Never varnish on excessively damp, foggy, or rainy days. Varnish applied in such conditions may take as long as a week to dry, compared with 6 to 8 hours in optimum conditions.

BRUSHING VARNISH

Applying varnish with a brush requires a somewhat specialized brushing technique. The first rule of applying a good varnish finish is not to skimp on the brush. Buy the finest quality soft-hair brushes you can obtain—the experts use fitch or badger brushes—and use them only for varnish, keeping them clean and in good shape. Inferior brushes will not hold and release the varnish at the proper rate. Also, they frequently shed bristles into the work.

A 2½-inch-wide brush is good for all but very delicate carvings. For intricate carvings on very detailed pieces, buy a ½-inch brush at an art-supply store. For pieces that have very large, flat surfaces, a 3-inch brush can speed work considerably, although a 2½-inch brush will generally take care of most home finishing jobs.

Varnish should be flowed onto the surface with as little brushing as possible. Overbrushing will cause the varnish to set up faster and can leave a surface with brush marks that will not flatten out as the surface dries.

To apply, dip the tip of the brush in a small quantity of varnish that has been poured into a clean, wide can or other suitable container. Always work with small quantities and keep the varnish can tightly closed. Always keep the brush well wetted with varnish. Cover a small area with a few strokes of the brush, letting the varnish flow evenly out of the brush in a thin coat. Then immediately go over the area, just barely touching the surface of the varnish with the tips of the bristles. These final strokes should always be directed into the area that has already been coated, not toward the edge of the surface yet to be covered. Some marks will probably still show on the surface but will soon flow out of their own accord if the varnish has been properly thinned and not excessively brushed. Then go on to another small area and repeat the operation. Avoid overlapping areas as much as possible and work quickly and steadily from one part of the piece to another.

Edges can be difficult. Always work from the center toward an edge. By brushing out over the edge, you will not squeeze varnish out of the brush which could cause excess finish to run off the edge.

On carved areas, let the brush follow the contours of the carving and do not worry about brushing in the direction of the grain. Use the brush properly and do not try to work varnish into crevices by jamming with the tip of the brush—this might save some time and brushwork but will leave a thick, uneven coat of varnish in the crevices.

Whenever possible work on horizontal surfaces. When it is necessary to varnish vertical surfaces, be especially careful not to pick up too much varnish on the brush in the first place, and try to apply as thin a coat as possible. Also, use downward strokes for the final leveling. This will prevent runs and sags. When a run or a sag does appear, brush in the direction of the run, using only enough pressure to even it out.

BUILDING UP A FINISH

A good varnish requires at least three coats over the sealer. One coat will never suffice and two are barely adequate. The finest finishes, like those used for pianos, have more than ten coats. A good finisher strives for four or five coats, each as thin as possible.

The coats should be allowed to dry thoroughly before proceeding. Coats should never be applied with less than 24 hours of drying time and 48 hours is even better. The old-time piano finishers sometimes allowed as long as 60 days drying between coats and the complete finishing job took as long as 8 months. If insufficient drying time is allowed, even the lightest sanding between coats will leave particles of abrasive embedded in the varnish. Since drying time varies according to temperature and humidity, it is a good idea to test for dryness before preparing to apply another coat. A simple test for dryness: press a fingernail into an inconspicuous part of the finished surface. If it leaves a mark, set the piece aside for further drying.

When the surface is fully dry, prepare for the next coat by sanding lightly with 220-grit abrasive paper. Barely go over the surface with light, even strokes; be extremely careful not to oversand. Obviously, too much sanding will remove or cut through the preceding coat. Sags or overthick areas near edges can be sanded out, but great care must be taken. Since these defects are so much thicker than the rest of the varnish coat, they take a much longer time to dry. If they are not completely dry, even the finest grade of sandpaper will cut into them deeply, leaving a depression and abrasive particles embedded in the finish. Such damage may necessitate stripping the surface and starting over. This, unfortunately, happens to amateurs and professionals alike. Allow at least 30 days before rubbing and polishing.

APPLYING VARNISH OVER OLD FINISHES

Old varnish finishes can be restored by varnishing over the old finish; a varnish finish can also be applied over an old shellac finish, both to restore it and to overcome shellac's poor resistance to moisture.

To apply varnish over an existing finish, remove all traces of oil, grease, wax, and dirt with a commercial de-waxing solution. Wiping with turpentine will also work, but is not quite as efficient as the store-bought products. Repair any nail holes, dents, or gouges with lacquer stick and sand the surface lightly with 220-grit sandpaper. Dust the piece thoroughly and apply a sealer coat of thinned varnish, let it dry overnight, sand again with 220 paper, and proceed as for bare wood.

Shellac

ABOUT SHELLAC

Shellac still has a place in wood finishing, even though its use has radically decreased since the development of varnish and more modern synthetic finishes. Shellac finishes are among the most beautiful available, having a gloss and clarity unequaled by almost any finishing material. The only possible exception is water white lacquer, a finish that is difficult to apply because spray equipment is essential. On the other hand, shellac is easily applied with a brush, dries quickly, picks up dust less readily than varnish, and is the easiest of all finishes to touch up or rejuvenate.

BUYING AND MIXING SHELLAC

Shellac is a hard natural resin that is secreted by a beetle that lives on trees in India. The resin is collected, melted, and purified, then solidified in flat, thin sheets that are broken up into flakes. The natural material has a red orange color but it is bleached to produce what is known as white shellac.

For use as a finish, the shellac resin is dissolved in alcohol. It is most frequently sold in dissolved form in hardware and paint stores. Dilution ranges from 2 to 5 pounds of shellac to 1 gallon of alcohol. Such dilutions are referred to as "cuts": 2 pounds of shellac in a gallon of alcohol is called a two-pound cut.

You can buy shellac in the form of resin flakes, but only in specialized paint stores and in other stores that cater to professional finishers. Even though it is much more expensive than the predissolved type (why it is, is just one of those mysteries) many professionals prefer to blend their own shellac. The reason is that shellac does not keep. As soon as it is dissolved in alcohol it begins a slow process of deterioration, becoming gummy and sticky, until it reaches a point at which it will not dry properly when applied to wood. For this reason, never buy premixed shellac that does not have a date marked on the can (most top-quality shellac is marked and only the best grades of shellac should be used on furniture). Never use shellac that is past its expiration date.

When mixing shellac from scratch, use only the purest alcohol. This is important, because excessive water in the alcohol, or the presence of oil, will ruin the shellac. It is a good idea to test the alcohol for purity before diluting, or "cutting," shellac. Take a sheet of good white bond paper and wet it with the alcohol. Since alcohol is very volatile, it should dry within a few minutes. Water will cause the paper to dry out slowly; oil will leave a greasy stain. Another simple test for oil is to pour some of the alcohol into a glass of water. The alcohol will mix with the water, but any oil present will float on the surface.

Mix the shellac flakes with alcohol, stirring thoroughly. For reference, it is easiest if the first mixing is always a four-pound cut, although two-pound cut, which is the best consistency for brush application, is also a good starting point. After stirring the flakes into the alcohol, let the mixture stand for several hours to allow the shellac to dissolve completely. There may be some solids that have settled to the bottom of the container. Stir these into the mixture and strain the shellac. An effective strainer for this purpose is a 10-inch length of nylon stocking tied at one end. Fix it over an open container, pour in the shellac, strain, and throw away the stocking. (To avoid danger of fire, place it on an old newspaper and let it air dry before throwing it into the trash.)

Both orange and white shellac are available commercially. While we recommend using only the best white shellac, some finishers occasionally use orange shellac to richen the color of the wood, particularly on dark woods. The drawback is that a number of coats may give too much color, obscuring the natural grain of the wood. For this reason, applying white shellac over stain is a more sensible approach that gives the finisher control over the final color no matter how many coats of shellac are applied.

Applying Shellac

Shellac, like other finishes, should always be applied over a properly prepared dust-free surface. Since shellac is so sensitive to moisture, a dry day or a low-humidity workplace is important. Like varnish, shellac should be applied at a temperature greater than 70° F. Since its solvent is alcohol, shellac dries much more rapidly than varnish; however, its volatility creates a greater fire hazard. Avoid open flames and work in a well-ventilated, but not drafty, area.

BRUSH APPLICATION

Two-pound-cut shellac is the best consistency for brush application. To make a two-pound, simply add an equal part of pure denatured alcohol to commercial four-pound-cut shellac. This will make a thin shellac that will brush easily, form a thin coat, and level out readily, so brush marks won't remain on the surface. Shellac should always be applied in a thin coat: if it is put on too thickly, cracks will form in the lower coats and eventually progress to the surface, producing an "alligator" effect.

Pour a small quantity of shellac into a small can or jar and seal the larger quantity promptly to prevent the alcohol from absorbing moisture from the air. If too much moisture is absorbed, the shellac will not dry properly and may whiten. Use a high-quality, soft-hair brush (a 2½-inch brush is adequate for most furniture work). Shellac should be applied with a full brush and a very light touch. Take a long sweeping stroke and then brush over it once with just the tips of the bristles to even out the largest brush marks. The shellac will level out very quickly.

Overbrushing will not help; it will only leave brush marks

on the surface. One reason is that since shellac dries very rapidly, especially when it is in a thin layer like that applied by a brush, it will dry under the brush. Another is that the alcohol in the coat being applied will soften the previous coat, allowing heavy brush strokes to disturb lower layers in the finish. The trick of getting a good, deep finish is to apply each coat without messing up the one before.

However, the solvent action does have an advantage. Since each coat partially dissolves the previous layer of finish, each coat is bonded to the next. For this reason, lap marks are less of a problem with shellac than with varnish. If an area is missed, rather than brushing over it, simply catch it on the next coat. Also, turnings and rungs can be coated on one side and then completed when the piece is dry enough to turn over.

Each coat should be allowed to dry for at least 8 hours before recoating. Between coats, lightly sand the surface with either 260-grit sandpaper or with size 0 steel wool to remove any surface roughness. Wipe thoroughly to remove sanding dust and steel-wool strands. Apply as many coats as you want; at least four are required for a good finish.

Because of evaporation, a small quantity of shellac may thicken while it is being used. Thin it to the proper consistency with alcohol. A good rule of thumb is to thin it until it flows on freely. If the brush starts to pull or drag, the shellac needs thinning; if the shellac runs, it has been thinned too much.

SPRAY APPLICATION

Like most other finishes, shellac can be applied by a spray gun. The exact viscosity will depend on the type of spray equipment used. For most finishing sprayers, the material should be at about a three-pound cut.

FRENCH POLISHING

French polishing is by far the most painstaking way of applying shellac, but one that, with hand rubbing, produces a finish that is incomparable in depth and luster. While it was probably perfected in France during the reign of Louis XV and was used mainly as a primary finishing technique for years afterward, these days it is used mostly in restoring old or damaged shellac finishes. It is a particularly good way to remove scratches and other types of minor damage from pieces without removing the entire finish. Aside from bare wood, French polishing can be used to apply shellac over almost any sound old finish including varnish, lacquer, or even paint, as long as the surface is clean and free from chalking.

Although extremely fine finishes can be built up from bare wood that has been stained and sealed, it is much easier to build up the finish with brush or spray, sanding between coats, and then apply a few final coats by hand rubbing.

The key to French polishing is good, old-fashioned elbow grease. A clean, lint-free cloth (linen or cheesecloth work best) is folded into a flat pad the size of a fist. Dip the pad into linseed oil (buy only boiled linseed oil) and then wring out all of the excess (the pad should be almost dry). In a dish (an old soup bowl is about the right size), pour some fresh, top-quality shellac at a two- to three-pound cut. Dip the pad into the shellac—it should be wet with shellac but not dripping.

Transfer the shellac from the pad to the wood by rubbing the surface with tight figure-eight or circular motions. The pad should move fairly rapidly over the surface, with just enough pressure to leave the surface wet with the thinnest possible coat of shellac. The proper pressure will come with practice, but it is essential that the pad never come to rest on the surface; it should be moved steadily and with even pressure from the time it comes in contact with the wood until it is removed to be refilled with shellac. If the pad begins to stick or drag, it is time to replenish the supply of shellac. If the pad seems to be losing its ability to surrender shellac, it probably means that it needs another wetting with linseed oil. This will be necessary from time to time as the work progresses. This is done by dipping it in oil and squeezing it out as in the beginning.

Allow the surface to dry at least 24 hours between coats, allowing more time as the finish builds up. Where the labor comes in is the number of coats—some fine old antique finishes may have as many as thirty coats, although ten is sufficient for most finishes. In fact, the very thick French-polished finishes sometimes have a rounded, plasticlike appearance because the wood is so thickly encased in shellac.

This method of applying shellac will produce a finish that looks like glass without a single ripple or open pore. In most cases, the surface will be too shiny for contemporary tastes, but it can be easily rubbed to a rich, lustrous satin finish (see Chapter 8).

Lacquer

ABOUT LACQUER

Modern lacquers, made from nitrocellulose, are resistant to water, alcohol, weak acids, and alkalis, and have a surface that is hard enough to resist wear but flexible enough not to become brittle and crack over long periods of time. As a finishing material, their only drawback is that they can be scratched fairly easily.

However, lacquer does have serious drawbacks for the amateur finisher. Because of the extremely volatile solvents that are used, it must be applied by spraying; if a brush is used, it can be applied only to relatively small areas. Its fast drying time becomes an asset in production-line work and, as a result, many pieces of modern furniture are finished with lacquers—a durable, good-looking finish can be applied in as little as two days. But the nonprofessional may find the timing a problem. Also, many finishers of fine antiques avoid lacquer because of the "hardness" of its appearance. It does not lend itself well to a deep, soft luster, which is prized on old wood, without a great deal of hand rubbing.

BUYING LACQUER

The first rule in selecting a lacquer is to be sure to obtain one formulated specifically for the intended purpose. There are many types of lacquer on the market, with uses ranging from fine wood to metal. These are accompanied by specialized thinners, which are *not* readily interchangeable.

Lacquers are available in gloss, satin, and flat grades and are made both for brushing and spraying. Satin and flat types contain flatting agents that labels claim produce a "hand-rubbed" effect, but like flatting agents added to varnish, they will produce a cloudy finish if they are used to build up a finish; they should only be used for the final coat, and even then, the results are inferior to those obtained by proper rubbing and polishing. The brushing lacquers have retarders added to the solvents which slow drying time somewhat but by no means enough to be comparable even to shellac.

APPLYING LACQUER BY BRUSH

On small surfaces, lacquer can be applied fairly successfully by brush, but on large flat areas like tabletops, only the most skilled craftsman can produce an acceptable finish. Brushing lacquer can be used with success on home woodwork, table legs, chairs, and small pieces of furniture such as commodes or boxes.

The critical thing to remember with brushing lacquer is to *flow* it onto the surface. It should be applied very thinly so there is no problem with leveling or brush marks, Since it dries almost instantly, any attempt at brushing over an already covered surface will only result in a mess. If an area is skipped, forget it and cover it with the next coat.

Proper brushing technique for lacquer is to use a top-quality soft-hair brush about 2 inches wide. Use a full brush and flow the finish on by moving the brush in one direction only. As soon as the brush begins to drag, return it for a fresh filling. Above all, move quickly. Allow at least 8 hours between coats, sand with 260-grit paper, dust carefully, and recoat. Allow the final coat to dry at least 24 hours before rubbing and polishing.

APPLYING LACQUER BY SPRAY

Lacquer lends itself much better to spray application. With only moderately good spray technique, it is possible to lay down nearly flawless coats.

Lacquer should be thinned for spraying, but the amount depends on the type of spray equipment used, the pressure, the temperature and humidity, and the experience of the operator. Because of the variables involved, it is almost impossible to give accurate guidelines; most finishers thin by instinct based on their experience. A basic rule of thumb, or at least a starting point, is to add about 30 percent thinner, see if it works, and, if not, add more thinner in small amounts until the material sprays well and coats properly.

One of the most common mistakes made by beginners spraying lacquer is not applying a thick enough coat. In order to avoid runs and sags (which indeed can be a problem), many novice sprayers will apply too fine a spray or move the spray gun too quickly over the surface. The result is a pebbly surface. A properly applied coat will leave the sprayed area looking wet, with a smooth, glassy appearance.

The secret of successful spraying is to apply as heavy a coat as possible without producing runs. If an occasional run should appear, it can sometimes be brushed out immediately with a soft brush. The run will probably still be visible on the dried surface but it can be sanded out: allow the coat to dry completely (about 8 hours) and sand with wet-or-dry silicon-carbide paper of 300 or 400 grit. Wet the paper and the surface with water. Always use a sanding block and be careful not to sand into the preceding coats. Even if the area is not perfectly smooth, don't sand too deep. Recoat the damaged area and sand a second time.

If slight ridges show up when the coated area is placed in a position in which it reflects light, smooth the surface lightly with 000 steel wool or 260-grit paper between coats.

After the final coat, allow at least 24 hours before rubbing or polishing.

Caution: Lacquer is mixed with volatile solvents. Always wear a charcoal respirator when spraying, and avoid breathing the fumes. The mixture is very flammable—work in a well-ventilated area away from any open flame.

COMPATIBILITY WITH OTHER FINISHES

Lacquer can be applied over lacquer or shellac but never over varnish or paint. The solvents in lacquer thinner will cause varnish to lift as surely as paint remover. As a result, shellac or lacquer sealer should be used before applying lacquer; and if lacquer is to be applied over an existing finish, give it a sealer coat of two-pound-cut shellac to prevent the lacquer thinner from penetrating to the old finish. While shellac will usually seal in an old finish, even varnish, this is still a risky procedure. If the surface is not perfectly sealed and lacquer thinner reaches a varnished surface, the finish will lift. When lifting occurs there is no alternative but to remove the old finish down to the bare wood and begin again.

Lacquer is also incompatible with oil. For this reason, many finishers who plan on applying a lacquer finish will use only water or alcohol stains and avoid oil stains. It is still possible to use an oil stain but the surface must be sealed either with a lacquer sealer that is compatible with both oil and lacquer or with shellac. If lacquer is applied directly over an oil stain, it will "alligator."

A whitening effect called blushing also sometimes occurs when lacquer is applied on too damp a day. It is caused by water vapor or oil becoming mixed into the lacquer. If the cause of blushing is moisture, applying a thin mist coat of lacquer thinner to the surface with a spray gun will usually clear it up. It will soften the surface enough to allow the water vapor to escape with the solvent. Another moisture problem is the formation of "fish eyes." These small circular blemishes are caused by moisture trapped in the lacquer. Moisture can be introduced into the lacquer during spraying on days when humidity is too high. There is no recourse but to remove the finish and start over again.

PADDING LACQUERS

Finishes called padding lacquers have recently been introduced on the market. They are not true lacquers and are compatible with varnish as well as shellac and other lacquers. If the surface is free of oil, grease, or wax, they bond well and produce an adequate finish. They can be applied by brush or spray to build up a finish. The final coats are applied by a pad in the manner of the French-polishing technique for shellac. They are also useful in making spot repairs on lacquered surfaces.

8

Rubbing and Polishing

The final step in finishing, particularly with clear finishes of shellac, varnish, or lacquer, is rubbing and polishing the finish to remove minute surface imperfections and to leave the finish with whatever degree of gloss or luster that is desired. This is accomplished by rubbing the surface with extremely fine abrasives; depending on the fineness of the abrasive, the finish can be brought up to a glasslike gloss or reduced to a rich, satiny luster. Indeed, few things in wood finishing can compare to a hand-rubbed finish. It produces the softness and richness that can otherwise be produced only by years of rubbing the hands over a piece of well-worn wood. The appearance is like that of an armchair that has been handled by generations of users or the handle of a well-used tool.

Both rubbing and polishing are essentially the same. The main difference is that rubbing requires more effort and generally reduces the gloss of the finish while removing embedded dust and dirt from the surface and smoothing off tiny ridges left in the finish by its application; polishing uses the finest possible abrasives and raises a finish dulled by rubbing to whatever level of gloss is required by the finisher. Polishing is easier; less time is required and less pressure is used on the abrasive.

Rubbing and polishing are so easy and versatile that it is pointless to buy commercial satin finishes. While a satin finish used as a final coat will leave a dull surface reminiscent of a hand-rubbed finish, surface imperfections and foreign contamination cannot be removed and, since the finish has dried to a predetermined gloss, the final effect cannot be controlled by the finisher. Furthermore, satin finishes are less transparent than gloss types, and thus obscure the grain of the wood beneath the finish. On the other hand, by working with clear gloss finishes and rubbing, the finisher has total control over the final outcome of the finish. If it is too glossy, it can be made duller; if rubbing reduces the gloss too much, it can easily be polished up to any degree of gloss.

Rubbing with Pumice

The abrasive used for rubbing is finely ground pumice, a glassy volcanic rock that can be very finely powdered. It is commercially available in six grades, ranging from coarse to fine. They are 1, 0, 0/½, 2/0, 3/0, and 4/0. Even the coarsest grades are much finer than the finest sandpaper. The coarser grades will leave a flat, dull finish; grades 2/0 and 3/0, a satiny "rubbed" finish; and the finest, 4/0, a slightly glossy "rubbed" finish.

Pumice is never used dry. Either water or oil is used to lubricate the surface during rubbing. For dull finishes, water is used; to achieve a higher gloss, oil is used. Since water provides less lubrication, the abrasive will cut faster and deeper. Because water lubricates less than oil, a comparable grade of pumice used with water will dull the surface more than the same grade with oil. For example, the appearance of the surface will be about the same when 4/0 pumice is used with water or 2/0 is used with oil. Oil, on the other hand, lubricates, so that the cutting action is both slower and less pronounced.

Rubbing Technique

Rubbing resembles sanding; the difference is that the grains of abrasive are not attached to a backing. In this case only *extremely* fine abrasives are used but the technique is the same as for sanding before sandpaper was invented.

Where fine sanding requires the use of a sanding block, rubbing is done with a thick felt or cloth pad, the most convenient size being 3 by 5 inches and 1 inch thick. Smaller pads are used for carvings and frets. Rubbing pads are sold in paint and refinishing-supply stores. As with sanding, rub with the grain, never across, and always use a straight motion with constant pressure, never a circular or figure-eight pattern. Occasionally, especially where marquetry or carvings have to be rubbed, a certain amount of cross-grain rubbing is unavoidable. In these cases use the finest grade of pumice (4/0) with oil and rub very gently. Take extra care on corners and sharp edges to avoid cutting completely through the finish.

Before rubbing, be absolutely sure that the surface is completely hard and dry, otherwise abrasive particles will become embedded in the surface and the finish may have to be removed. Also, if a finish is rubbed too soon, hairline cracks may appear in it. They are the result of scratching the surface before it is completely dry; these scratches allow the finish to pull apart as it shrinks during the drying. When this happens, the cracks can usually be rubbed out but it is simple enough to avoid this and far easier than having to rub a piece twice.

Allow at least 30 days of good drying before rubbing varnish; 2 weeks for shellac; and 48 hours for lacquer.

RUBBING WITH OIL

Pumice is usually used with crude oil or commercially prepared rubbing oil, which can be purchased at paint stores that also sell pumice. Some finishers also use 10-weight motor oil or paraffin oil, but commercial rubbing oils are generally the best. They are formulated so that they will not become gummy with rubbing and so that the heat produced in rubbing will not cause them to penetrate and soften the finish. In fact, overly vigorous rubbing that generates a lot of frictional heating should be avoided.

Fill a shallow container (an old pie plate is good) with rubbing oil, another with pumice. Sprinkle pumice over the surface of the finish and then sprinkle the surface with oil. Dip the felt pad into the oil and begin rubbing. Through trial and error you will learn how much oil and pumice to use. The best results are obtained when the mixture of oil and pumice on the surface is about the consistency of thin pancake batter. If the mixture is too thin, the cutting action will be minimal; too thick, the mixture will stick together and not cut at all.

Continue rubbing, using even strokes and constant pressure, until all ridges and surface irregularities have been removed and the surface has reached the desired luster. The smoothness of the surface should be checked frequently by wiping it clean with a fingertip or the side of the hand.

Use additional pumice and oil from time to time as the mixture thickens up and loses its cutting ability. If a duller or shinier surface is desired, switch to a coarser or finer grade of pumice.

RUBBING WITH WATER

The technique for using water is essentially the same as for oil. The main difference is that the abrasive will cut faster so that more frequent inspection and lighter pressure on the pad make sense. Also, since water evaporates, sprinkle the surface from time to time to keep the abrasive properly lubricated.

With water rubbing, a soft sheen can be obtained by switching from the rubbing pad to a soft, lint-free cloth. This will reduce the abrasive action further and have the effect of polishing the surface. Do not use water as a pumice lubricant on a shellac finish—it will ruin it.

Cleaning Up After Rubbing

After using pumice, all traces must be removed before polishing by washing. Clear water and soft cloths are usually adequate, although some finishers prefer a solution of lukewarm soapy water. When oil has been used as a lubricant, it is every bit as important to remove it along with the residue of pumice. Oil left on the surface will cause the finish to become hazy and may soften it. Shellac will stand water for a short period of time but wash the surface quickly and wipe up immediately with clean dry cloths.

Once the finish has attained the desired gloss, give it a final wipe with a good furniture polish. This will clean off any remaining traces of pumice and oil and will protect the rubbed finish. Rubbed satin finishes can also be treated with paste wax for final cleanup and protection. Apply a good paste wax with a soft cloth.

Polishing with Rottenstone

While pumice can be used to produce finishes ranging in luster from dull to satin, it is not a fine enough abrasive to leave a high-gloss finish. For a high gloss, another mineral abrasive called rottenstone is used. It is extremely fine and will produce a glasslike mirror surface that is even glossier than an untreated final coat of high-gloss finish.

Rottenstone is used in the same way as pumice and is really nothing more than a continuation of the polishing procedure begun with pumice. However, at least a week should be allowed between pumice rubbing and rottenstone polishing to allow the finish to harden up after being exposed to oil during rubbing.

Never use the same pad with rottenstone and pumice. Pumice particles stuck in the pad will defeat your purpose. Also, rottenstone is never used with water as a lubricant, always with oil. For an extremely high gloss, some finishers use their hand instead of a felt pad for the final rubbing. After polishing with rottenstone, clean up with water and emulsion polish. Wax will reduce the sheen of very high-gloss finishes; if you want the high gloss, finish with furniture polish.

Rubbing and Polishing Compounds

While the traditional methods of rubbing and polishing with pumice and rottenstone are still preferred by many finishers, newer, premixed rubbing compounds are replacing them in many shops. There are pastes made of abrasives of various finenesses. They are applied directly from the can and, as they are rubbed, they dry out, leaving a stiff residue that can be easily removed with emulsion-type furniture polish on a damp cloth. As the compound dries, the abrasive action is reduced, leaving a highly polished surface. If the compound dries completely and the surface has still not reached the desired gloss, remove the residue and add more compound. Continue rubbing until the surface is satisfactory.

Rubbing compounds are recommended for rubbing and polishing lacquer finishes. Although pumice and rottenstone can be used, the abrasives in the commercial compounds are much harder and will cut faster on lacquer finishes, some of which are extremely hard.

Rubbing compounds come in a number of grades, according to the fineness of the abrasive, and the proper compound should be selected for flat, satin, or polished finishes.

Shortcuts with Sandpaper and Steel Wool

In extreme cases, some finishes are too hard to be easily rubbed even with rubbing compounds. Included are some of the synthetic enamels, baking enamels, and porcelain enamels. The only practical way to give the finished surface a final rubbing is to use sandpaper. These may be sanded with 400- or 500-grit wet-or-dry sandpaper lubricated with rubbing oil that has been slightly thinned with mineral spirits.

Such techniques can also be used as shortcuts to rubbing and polishing. But these will never equal a hand-rubbed finish. And, if a finer finish is desired, hand rubbing is still necessary. A very high-gloss finish can only be obtained with rottenstone and oil.

If a satin finish is desired, 400-grit paper with oil and thinner is an acceptable shortcut. The danger is oversanding and cutting too deeply into the finish. Sand only enough to produce a smooth satin finish—check the work carefully and stop as soon as the surface is free of imperfections and irregularities.

Another shortcut instead of rubbing is to sand the final coat with 400-grit paper without lubrication and then apply a good-quality paste wax with 000 or 0000 steel wool. The wax-impregnated steel wool will polish out the rough spots, leaving a smooth satin finish. Coarser steel wool can be used to leave a less glossy finish.

9

Oil and Wax Finishes

Two of the oldest finishes for wood, as well as the easiest to maintain and most durable, are oil and wax finishes. Unlike shellac, varnish, and lacquer, these finishes are virtually fail-safe: they can be applied in fits and starts, can be touched up at any time without showing repairs, and are as resistant to wear and damage as other common finishes.

What they have in common is that they require lots of elbow grease to apply. Coat after coat is rubbed into the wood until the finishing material has impregnated the fibers of the wood. But the work pays off in lustrous finishes that are among the most beautiful provided by any wood-finishing technique.

The durability of both oil and wax finishes is the root of their one drawback: they are almost impossible to remove because of the depth to which they penetrate the wood. They are not touched by paint removers, although they could be removed by laborious sanding that would leave a piece of furniture considerably thinner than it was originally. Oil finishes, however, can be sanded slightly and coated with varnish; wax finishes can be neither removed nor recoated—the wax will prevent any finish coat from adhering to the wood.

Oil Finishes

A well-applied oil finish has all of the attributes desirable in a finish. It is resistant to impact, heat, alcohol, and abrasion. In its simplest form, an oil finish consists of applying coat after coat of boiled linseed oil to the wood, rubbing in each coat and letting it dry thoroughly before a subsequent coat is applied. However, pure oil is rarely used. Finishers use a mixture of oil and turpentine, usually mixed in equal parts. The turpentine thins out the oil and enables it to penetrate the wood more readily. When the turpentine evaporates, the oil remains in the wood.

A variation that is the easiest to apply and makes for the most durable oil finish involves adding varnish to the linseed-oil and turpentine mixture. With a mixture consisting of 1 part boiled linseed oil, 1 part turpentine, and 1 part good furniture varnish, the oil will penetrate deeply into the wood without forming a skin, and a thin coat of varnish will remain on the wood after each application. The result is a lasting permanent finish with a rich luster that can be touched up with the same mixture if it is damaged.

On the other hand, when linseed oil is used without the addition of varnish, recoating at least once a year is necessary to maintain the appearance of the finish. Another drawback of linseed oil without varnish is that it will become dull and requires a lot of buffing to maintain its gloss. And, unless the wood is well seasoned, it will sweat oil during hot weather, leaving a gummy layer on the surface that will attract dust and must be wiped off with turpentine.

Applying Oil Finishes

Oil finishes must be applied only to wood that is completely free of any old finish or wax that could block the absorption of the oil. For this reason, oil finishes are frequently used as a low-cost method of finishing commercial "unfinished furniture."

If the surface is to be stained, staining should take place at least two weeks before oiling begins to allow the stain to dry thoroughly. Before staining, it is a good idea to oil a small concealed portion of the piece to get an idea of the effect of oiling on the wood. Oil will darken the wood somewhat and this effect should be taken into consideration when a stain is selected.

After staining, smooth the surface of the wood with 220-grit sandpaper, wipe the surface clean with a lint-free rag, and apply the first coat of oil mixture. Apply the oil liberally with a brush (a rag can also be used) and allow it to soak into the wood for 10 to 20 minutes. Wipe off the excess with a clean rag. Some finishers prefer to rub the oil into the wood, using a cloth, 000 steel wool, or the bare hand. The rubbing action generates heat, making the oil flow more easily into the pores of the wood and actively forcing the oil into the wood. When the oil has been worked well into the wood, wipe off any excess remaining on the surface with a clean lint-free rag and set the piece aside to dry for at least 72 hours before recoating. The piece is sufficiently dry when the smell of turpentine is no longer detectable.

Once the first coat of oil has been applied and allowed to dry, the piece can be put into normal use and oiled at leisure, allowing at least two weeks to a month between coats thereafter. Three coats is the bare minimum, but deciding when to stop is entirely up to the finisher. This is a finish that gains depth and luster as more and more coats are applied and one that cannot be spoiled by improper application. If the oil is left on too long, it can be cleaned up with turpentine and a soft rag. If you stop in the middle of applying a coat, it can be completed at any time without creating lap marks or color differences, and missed spots can be covered up by the next coat.

The oil mixture should be stored in a tightly capped jar to prevent the turpentine from evaporating. A mason jar with a metal screw top makes a good storage container. When applying the oil mixture, pour only what you need into a small container and recap the main supply to minimize evaporation. Even so, the mixture may become gummy as turpentine evaporates; this can be corrected by adding small amounts of turpentine from time to time.

When you decide the finish is the way you want it (or when you get tired of applying additional coats), the surface may be waxed with a good paste wax. As with the application of the oil, the wax should be rubbed vigorously to produce a soft luster. Another somewhat laborious way to improve the luster of the piece is to rub the surface with the palm of your hand between coats. Rub until your hand begins to feel hot and then move on to another place. This will result in a satin smoothness that cannot be duplicated by any other means.

Commercial Oil Finishes

In recent years, commercial finishes broadly called "oil finishes" have appeared on the market. Their advent coincided with the popularity of Danish-style furniture and the demand among professional and amateur wood finishers for products that would produce what was popularly called a "Danish oil finish."

These finishes are based on a number of materials, including tung oil (a natural oil, derived from the Chinese tung tree, that is known for its hardness and penetrating ability) and synthetic resins such as the urethanes. For the most part, they are similar to the extremely hard floor finishes developed for gymnasiums. As a class of finishes, they have become known as penetrating wood sealers and many are good finishes for furniture.

Nonetheless, the products sold as "oil finishes" are not oil finishes in the true sense. Rather, they are wood sealers that, unlike a traditional oil finish, usually produce a finish that is dead flat, leaving the texture of the wood completely exposed. While the application of several coats will begin to build up a satiny appearance, they will never equal the rich sheen of a hand-rubbed oil finish.

They are, however, true wood finishes: they seal and protect the wood from damage. They harden the surface of the wood and are, in many cases, very resistant to heat and solvents, such as alcohol. They are washable, being very resistant to water, and can be recoated at any time. They are good finishes for unpainted furniture, wall paneling, doors, woodwork, and interior trim, although they do not match the beauty of the more traditional finishing techniques for fine antique furniture.

There are many products on the market and a bewildering array of formulations, with both high-quality and inferior finishes being manufactured. The best bet is to stick to products of leading manufacturers and follow the maker's instructions closely.

Wax Finishes

Rubbing coat after coat of wax into raw wood is probably one of the oldest wood-finishing methods. It requires the least skill of any finishing method but makes up for it by the amount of time required for repeated waxing and buffing. However, this finish is easy to maintain—just add another coat of wax—and it has a rich, soft sheen that is attractive on

old pine and primitive furniture. Wax finishes are fairly resistant to abrasion and wear, depending on the quality of the
wax.

About Furniture Waxes

The waxes commonly used on furniture are sold in paste, liquid, and emulsion form. The paste waxes are blends of various waxes with a solvent such as turpentine or mineral
spirits. Liquid waxes contain more solvent, which provides a
cleaning action while laying down a thin layer of wax. The
emulsion polishes, used only on finished furniture, contain
soaps and detergents as well as some water. They are used
where it is necessary to clean accumulated dirt from finished
wood.

Only the best quality paste waxes should be used for wax
finishes or for applying an initial coat of wax to newly finished wood. Most commercial waxes are blends of various
natural waxes. The best ones contain up to 50 percent carnauba wax, which is derived from a South American palm
tree and is sometimes called Brazil wax. Carnauba wax is the
hardest natural wax known and produces the most durable
wax layer on wood. However, it is also very brittle and difficult to rub smooth, so it is never used by itself but is blended with other waxes. A common blending wax is beeswax.
Other waxes sometimes used include cadelilla, a vegetable
wax similar to beeswax, and ceresin, a wax obtained from
petroleum distillation, which is very durable and has a melting point close to that of carnauba wax. Paraffin, another
wax produced from petroleum, is soft and has a low melting
point. It is used in poor-quality furniture waxes.

The best waxes should be used for wax finishes. Waxes

can be colored by melting them and then adding oil stains. For most work, however, it is easier to stain the wood before waxing. To obscure unpleasant grain effects or give a fake-antique appearance to a wax finish, a small quantity of rottenstone can be added to the wax. The rottenstone produces a cloudy, opaque finish.

Applying a Wax Finish

The original wax finishes were simply successive coats of beeswax rubbed into the wood by hand. The natural temperature of the hand combined with the frictional heat produced by rubbing would blend the wax into the wood in a fine, even coat. The application of each coat would remove dirt and soften the previous coats of wax slightly to form a bond with the underlying layers.

A similar finish can be achieved without quite so much work by applying at least two coats of oil finish and then commencing with wax. An alternative technique is to seal the wood with shellac before waxing, but the interaction of oil and wax seems to produce a better finish.

Stain the wood, apply an initial coat of oil, and allow it to dry for at least 72 hours. Apply the additional coats of oil in the same way. Allow between 3 and 6 weeks for the oil to penetrate thoroughly and dry. Then apply a coat of top-quality paste wax.

The best way to apply paste wax is to make a pad out of a square foot of either cheesecloth or a close-textured cloth such as linen. In fact, an old napkin or handkerchief works very well. The first coat of wax should be thinned slightly so that it can be worked deep into the pores of the wood. When using commercial paste wax, either add a small amount of turpentine and allow it to sit overnight or heat the wax slightly in a pan of warm water to soften it. Since heating avoids the addition of turpentine, which will have to evaporate before the wax can be polished, it is the preferred method.

With a waxing pad (or just a wax-coated cloth the way you would polish shoes, if you prefer) apply an even coat of wax to the surface, using a circular motion. Hard rubbing is the key to this step; frictional heat and pressure will force it into the wood and bring the wax up to a fine polish.

Allow the wax to harden for at least a week, then apply another coat in the same manner—thinning the wax with turpentine is not necessary after the first coat. Follow with three or four waxings at intervals of five to six weeks to produce a lasting finish that will require only an occasional waxing and buffing to maintain its lustrous sheen. To bring the surface to a final high polish, use a soft cloth, rubbing briskly with the maximum pressure you can apply. When the wax has been properly rubbed, it will not show a print if a finger or thumb is pressed against the surface. If a fingerprint shows, more rubbing is necessary. There are no shortcuts possible with a waxed finish. The only way to achieve the rich, hand-rubbed luster is by vigorous rubbing and a lot of pressure. On flat surfaces, placing a brick on top of a soft cloth pad can provide additional pressure for the rubbing.

A wax finish can be applied faster if the wood is first sealed with either shellac or a penetrating wood sealer. This will close the pores of the wood, making it less absorbent to wax and permitting the wax to build up faster on the surface. While the wax will not be bonded as well to the wood as when it is applied over either bare or oiled wood, it is still a durable finish if the wax is properly applied with the requisite amount of brisk rubbing.

A wax finish requires little maintenance. An occasional buffing with a soft cloth, and an additional coat of wax once a year is all that is necessary. If the finish becomes water-marked or scratched, it can be repaired by applying wax with a pad of 000 steel wool, then buffing and repolishing the affected area. If too much wax is applied or if wax forms lumps on the surface, it can be almost impossible to rub it smooth. If this happens, excess can be removed by rubbing with a 000 steel-wool pad that contains a small amount of new wax. After rubbing off the excess with steel wool, buff the surface with a coarse cloth.

Commercial Wax Finishes

A number of commercial wax finishes are now on the market. Once again, these are not true wax finishes but are mixtures of stain, solvents, and wax. They are designed for the inexperienced finisher and the end result cannot be compared to a properly applied wax finish, which is not all that difficult to do in any case.

Like the commercial oil finishes, they are suitable for applying a fast, light-duty finish to unfinished furniture, wood paneling, and interior trim.

10

Enameling and Painting

One of the joys of furniture refinishing is to strip off layers of old paint from a nondescript piece of furniture to expose the rich mellowness of fine old wood. But what if removing the old finish bares a patchwork of filled dents and holes, low-quality wood with undistinguished grain, or inept repairs?

A possible solution is to give the whole thing up for a bad job, get another piece, and start over. Another is to accept the wisdom of the person who painted it in the first place. Finishers are frequently overly hasty in snubbing paint as a finish. True, a lot of very fine old furniture has been covered by paint over the years, and there are few more gratifying experiences in furniture refinishing than liberating a graceful, finely made piece of furniture maker's art from a cocoon of cracked gray porch paint. On the other hand, though, much furniture was made to be painted—fine wood was not used, grain was not matched. The intention was simply to make a serviceable, utilitarian piece of furniture. In some cases, this furniture was used in its raw, unfinished state; in others, it was painted to give it a durable, lasting protective coating; and sometimes it was elaborately decorated with painted designs and patterns.

Examples of painted furniture range from the black Boston

rocker—many of which could be remarkably attractive if covered with clear finish, but which tradition dictates be left with their original black finish and stencils—to elaborately decorated Eastern European peasant furniture, which loses almost all of its value if the original paint is removed.

Whether or not paint is called for by the piece itself, it is a valid finish in its own right. That paint is a durable, easily maintained finish can be attested to by anyone who has removed fifteen or twenty coats from an old piece of furniture. Paint has all the attributes of the best clear finishes: it is flexible and resists cracking, has good resistance to abrasion and wear, withstands alcohol and water, and, above all, can be a very attractive, colorful finish.

Selecting Paints and Enamels

Paints and enamels are formulated for a vast range of purposes and characteristics: interior and exterior, floors and walls, wood and metal, fast drying and slow drying, and so on. And with each it is necessary to use the proper primer or undercoat designed for use with the particular paint.

Enamels are usually regarded as the most durable and best suited to furniture and similar wood-finishing applications. They are harder and less spongy than other paints and, unlike exterior house paints, are formulated so that they do not "chalk." Chalking, the formation of a thin layer of powder on the surface, provides a self-cleaning property for exterior house paints but is not the kind of thing most people would appreciate in a furniture finish.

The enamels that are suitable for wood finishing come in several different types. A powdered type of enamel that is mixed with alcohol is very similar to high-quality lacquers and is used by expert finishers for touch-ups and certain special applications. But the most common are the plastic or synthetic enamels. These are made for a variety of purposes and are formulated for both air drying and baking. The baking types come in commercial grades that require high heat and huge baking ovens, and in low-heat grades that require from a half hour to an hour of heating at about 200° F. These latter can be used on furniture and allowed to air dry, but they form a harder, more durable finish if baked. They can be used by the home finisher, however. Small pieces can be baked in the home oven and large pieces can be heated under infrared lamps, although these represent a significant investment to a finisher who enamels infrequently.

The synthetic enamels, at least the higher-quality ones, are also formulated for the method of application and have different solvents and viscosities, according to whether they are intended for spraying, brushing, or dipping. Drying times vary from 15 minutes, for the types used by sign painters and sold in spray cans for touch-up, to 4 or 8 hours. Newer synthetic enamels based on urethane are the type commonly sold in hardware stores, grocery stores, and variety stores. They do not provide a hard, high-quality finish.

If all that seems confusing, it is because commercial enamels vary widely. If you plan to apply a lasting, durable finish, buy your enamel at a paint store and be careful to select a good product that is made specifically for wood finishing and has been formulated for the type of application you intend. Undercoats or primers are essential to a good job, and these too are made for specific purposes. Always buy the same brand of undercoat, and use thinners recommended by the manufacturer.

While enamels are available in both gloss and flat types, the best approach to a satin enamel finish is to apply gloss enamel and rub it down with pumice and oil. In this way the final gloss of the finish can be controlled by the finisher, not the paint manufacturer.

Applying Enamel Finishes

In some respects, enamel finishes are easier to apply than clear finishes like varnish or shellac. Their solid color masks uneven coating; runs and sags (if they form) can be sanded out and easily recoated without any danger of the repair showing; and missed areas are easy to spot.

Yet achieving the glassy smoothness of a fine enamel finish involves much more than brushing on some paint. Like any fine wood finish, the final surface will only be as smooth as the surface it is applied to. Raw wood should be sanded smooth with 220-grit sandpaper and sealed with two-pound-cut shellac; open-grained wood should be sealed, filled with paste wood filler, resanded, and sealed once more.

A good brush should be used for both the primer coat and the final coats of enamel. The material should be flowed on evenly, brushing in the direction of the grain to produce a thin, even coat. But avoid excessive brushing that will prevent the enamel from leveling itself out, leaving brush marks that will show after the finish has dried. The enamel should be thinned with the proper, high-grade thinner to form a smooth, even coat but not thinned so much that it runs out of the brush.

The primer should be allowed to dry thoroughly, sanded with 220-grit paper, and followed by from one to several topcoats of enamel. Sanding with 220-grit paper should precede each coat after the previous one has been allowed to dry completely. The label on an enamel can will tell you that the enamel dries in 4 hours, 8 hours, or even 1 hour, but enamels are almost never hard enough to sand in that time, even though they may be dry to the touch. A good rule of thumb is to allow at least eight times the time specified before sanding. The reason of course is that enamels do not sand very well, and if they are the least bit gummy, they will clog the paper and become scratched by the sanding.

As with other finishes, enamels should be applied at temperatures above 70° F and on days with low humidity. While the faster-drying types minimize problems with air-borne dust, working in a dust-free environment guarantees a better job and minimizes the amount of sanding required between coats.

If runs and sags develop after the finish has begun to set, brush lightly in the direction of the run, but do not attempt to brush it out completely. After the surface dries, sand the rough spots with 280-grit sandpaper and water, then allow it to dry thoroughly before applying the next coat.

If you wish to paint an old finished surface, first make sure that it is basically sound. The enamel finish you apply will be no more durable than what's under it. If an old finish is severely cracked or alligatored, it is better to remove it completely and start from bare wood. On the other hand, if an old finish is simply marred and worn but solid, it can easily be coated with enamel.

The first step to enameling over an old finish is to remove all wax and dirt from the surface. A commercial dewaxing solution or a turpentine-soaked rag are adequate in most cases. A surface that is covered by flaky old paint or powdery varnish can be washed with a solution of trisodium phosphate (TSP) in hot water. This will remove wax, dirt, and old disintegrated paint or varnish.

After cleaning, the piece should be sanded thoroughly with 80-grit sandpaper to remove any rough spots and smooth all surfaces. Touch up any bare spots with undercoat, fill any holes or gouges with wood putty, and sand smooth. Then coat the entire piece with undercoat and sand with 220-grit sandpaper. Proceed with enamel.

When the enamel has been built up to the desired thickness and allowed to dry thoroughly, it can be rubbed with pumice, rubbing compound, or 280-grit paper.

"Antiquing" or Glazing with Enamels

In the same way that glazing stains are used with clear finishes to create highlights, contrasting enamels can be used to produce special effects on painted furniture. The process is commonly called "antiquing," although there is nothing antique about it. It is a relatively new idea that achieved fad popularity not too long ago and was never used on old furniture.

A base coat of enamel, applied as in the preceding section, is covered with a "glaze" of contrasting color. Most of the glaze is wiped off, leaving only traces in the low spots of the grain, in the hollows of turnings and decorative carvings, and at the edges of the flat surfaces to provide a vignetted effect. Selection of the colors to be used is the most important step. It must be remembered that the final effect will be a color somewhere in between the color of the base coat and that of the glaze. For example, if a bold red base coat is glazed with white, the end result will be pink. Likewise, if a black or dark brown glaze is used, the final effect will be to darken the base color. Because the glaze has the effect of softening the base color, base coats should be very bright, bold colors. Some possible combinations are green and blue, yellow and brown, red and black, yellow and white.

Antiquing works best on open-grained, new wood although it can be done on almost any surface. If a piece is to be antiqued, the wood need not be filled first, since it is the small pores in the grain that will retain the glazing color after most of the glaze is wiped off. The piece should be given one or two coats of base enamel, allowed to dry, and lightly sanded with 280-grit sandpaper. It is a good idea, when applying the base coat, to enamel part of the underside or some concealed surface to practice glazing. Glazing coats dry very slowly so that they can be wiped off completely to vary the intensity of the color until a pleasing combination is achieved.

The glaze is a slow-drying oily liquid into which tinting colors have been mixed. Glazing liquid can be purchased at paint stores or made as needed. In fact, many paint stores package antiquing kits that consist of a base enamel and a premixed glaze; it is just as easy to purchase enamel and glaze separately. If you do it yourself, the color combinations are limited only by your imagination.

Commercial glazing liquids are clear mixtures of oil and driers formulated to dry slowly. They are colored either with dry colors or with oil-based tinting colors that can be bought at good paint stores. Mix glaze in small amounts: less than a cupful is sufficient for a chest of drawers or a table. A good basic recipe for mixing glaze is to thin about a tablespoonful of color-in-oil in about ¼ cup of turpentine or mineral spirits Mix thoroughly until the pigment is evenly dispersed in the thinner, then add about a cupful of glazing liquid and continue stirring until the color is evenly mixed.

To prepare a glaze from scratch, mix a tablespoonful of oil colors in a ¼ cup of turpentine or mineral spirits. Add 1 tablespoon of Japan drier or 2 tablespoons of clear furniture varnish and mix thoroughly.

The mixed glaze will appear much darker in the can than it will when it is applied over the enamel base. To see if it achieves the desired effect, brush a small amount onto a hidden test area. (If you did not enamel a small hidden area for practice, try out the glaze on an inconspicuous area. It can easily be completely removed with a rag dampened with turpentine or paint thinner.) Cover the test area completely with the glaze: the brushing job need not be perfect, brush strokes can be haphazard and visible, but the entire surface should be coated. After about 10 minutes wipe off the glaze with a clean piece of cheesecloth. Wipe carefully so that some of the glaze remains in the pores and grain of the wood. If the glaze is too light, add more tinting color; if it is too dark, thin it with turpentine or mineral spirits. Remove all the glaze from the test area by wiping with a turpentine-soaked rag, wipe the area dry with a dry cloth, and try again.

When the proper color has been achieved, begin glazing the piece. Unless the object to be glazed is quite small, the best approach is to glaze a single surface at a time. This will allow the glaze to be wiped off and the color blended without any part of the work becoming too dry. Brush on a heavy, fairly even coat of the glaze. Allow the glaze to set for 10 to 15 minutes, until it has become somewhat dull. The object is for the glaze to have dried only enough so that most, but not all, will wipe off. If a light wiping seems to be removing all the glaze, it has not set sufficiently. Most glazes will stay workable for at least half an hour. After a couple of tries, the proper time to begin wiping should be obvious. And, in any case, glazing is a very forgiving process: if you don't like the results, remove all the glaze with a turpentine-soaked rag and try again. Imperfections can be corrected by brushing a second coat of glaze on specific areas and blending it into the surrounding area by wiping.

A pad of clean cheescloth is the best material for wiping and blending the glaze, although squares of burlap or other lint-free rags will also work. On flat surfaces, begin wiping the glaze with short strokes starting in the center and working toward the edges. When the pad becomes clogged with excess glaze, fold it to expose a clean surface. By moving the glaze from the center toward the edge, you'll leave more glaze at the edges, giving an appearance of "depth." If desired, the glaze can be blended further by brushing it out with a paint brush, working from the center to the edge. Wipe the brush frequently on a clean rag so that it is picking up glaze rather than just moving it around. On turnings, such as legs and chair rungs, and on carved surfaces, wiping with the cheesecloth will remove most of the glaze from the high areas while leaving more in the depressions. Thick pools of glaze in the depressions of carvings should be removed with a small, dry paintbrush.

Although the piece can be used as soon as the glaze has thoroughly dried—allow at least 48 hours—it is a good idea to protect the glaze with a coat of clear furniture varnish. Test a small area to make sure that the varnish is compatible with the enamel and glaze—the glaze should not dissolve in the varnish and the varnish should bond to the enamel. Then give the whole piece a thin, even coat of varnish. The varnish may be left as is or rubbed to the desired gloss. If you prefer not to go to the additional step of varnishing, protect the surface with a coat of good furniture wax.

Pickled, Limed, and Blond Finishes

Like antiquing, so-called pickled and limed finishes reached fad proportion and now have faded into relative disuse. They were popular as a finish for the heavy "Spanish" and "mission" furniture styles. They, and the related blond finishes, still hold an important place in commercial finishes for such things as store counters and wall paneling.

Their main virtue is that they can be used to dress up inferior wood or make it look like a wood that it is not. By using paints and wood toners, the character of the wood is obscured or drastically altered. In most cases, all the natural color is removed from the wood by very heavy bleaching; or the natural color is hidden by the use of wood toners— brushable, heavily pigmented materials whose properties fall between those of a thin paint and a heavy pigmented oil stain. They are applied in the same way as stains. The most commonly available toners simulate the appearances of bleached wood and are used in commercial finishes to avoid the lengthy process of bleaching. They are available in such "bleached" shades as driftwood, maple, wheat blond, and bleached mahogany.

A pickled finish is simply wood that has been filled with a white pigment, usually paint. When the wood has been bleached before filling, the finish is referred to as "limed." Pickling and liming are most dramatic on open-grained woods with large pores that hold the white pigment, such as oak and mahogany. However, pickled pine finishes were once very popular. In some cases, the wood was given an initial dark stain to accentuate the white pigment in the open areas of the grain.

To apply a pickled finish, the wood is first stained, if desired, and then sealed with a coat of two-pound-cut shellac. After the shellac has dried thoroughly, sand it lightly with 220-grit sandpaper. Enamel is then applied in the same manner as in glazing. The enamel, usually white although other light colors can be used, should be thinned with the appropriate thinner to about half its usual consistency. Brush the enamel onto the piece roughly but thoroughly, covering an area that can be easily worked at one time. Do *not* allow the paint to set; begin wiping it off with a pad of clean cheese-cloth immediately. The paint should be wiped in the same manner as wood fillers (see p. 128), working across the grain with short strokes to pack the pigment into the pores and open-grained areas of the wood.

After the paint has dried thoroughly, protect it with several coats of a clear finish. The preferred finish for pickled, limed, and other blond finishes is water-white lacquer.

Be careful: Since enamel and lacquer are not compatible, the surface must first be sealed with a wash coat of two-pound-cut shellac. Most other finishing materials, even though they are sold as clear finishes, have too much color to produce a totally "blond" finish. Some of the newer varnishes and synthetics are acceptable, but even these have a slight yellow orange cast that can be observed by looking into the full can—and they tend to darken somewhat with age.

The final finish can be rubbed, polished, or waxed to taste. When the paint has dried, rub the surface with 000 steel wool to remove any traces of pigment that remain on the high areas, leaving only the pigment in the pores and grain.

Limed finishes are accomplished in the same way, except that they are applied over wood, frequently oak, that has been bleached as light as possible. Powerful wood bleaches, the two-part formulations, are used. Toners can be used as a shortcut to bleaching, or the bleached wood can be stained with a silvery gray stain after bleaching to lighten it still further. Following bleaching or staining, the wood should be sealed with water-white or clear lacquer (if a lacquer finish is planned) or with two-pound-cut shellac. Sand with 220-grit sandpaper, fill with white enamel or a white paste wood filler, let it dry overnight, and proceed with the final finish.

A number of other blond finishes are variations on the pickled and limed finishes. By starting with bleached or toned wood and adding color in the form of fillers, various effects—bearing little or no relationship to the natural appearance of the wood—can be obtained. Some of the more common blond finishes are:

Blond Oak. Bleached oak or oak treated with bleached-mahogany wood toner is sealed with water-white lacquer and allowed to dry overnight. The wood is filled with natural-oak-color paste wood filler, which is allowed to dry and then is sealed. Build up a final finish of water-white lacquer, sanding with 220-grit paper between coats.

Wheat Mahogany. Bleach and seal the wood or apply one or two coats of bleached-mahogany wood toner and seal after allowing to dry overnight. Fill with a wheat-colored filler (can be purchased or made by tinting natural filler lightly with raw sienna). When the filler has dried, seal and build up a final finish with several coats of water-white lacquer, sanding between coats with 220-grit sandpaper.

Heather Mahogany. The wood is either bleached or treated with a coat or two of bleached-mahogany wood toner and then sealed. It is then filled with either white enamel or white wood filler, sealed with water-white lacquer, and finished with several coats of lacquer.

Honey-Tone Maple. Since most varieties of maple are very light, bleaching can be omitted. Stain with honey-maple stain and seal (if oil stain is used, seal with two-pound-cut shellac). Finish with water-white lacquer.

11

Restoring, Repairing, and Maintaining Wood Finishes

With proper care, fine finishes will improve with age. Their luster will deepen and they will develop a soft, rich patina. But, unfortunately, few furniture finishes ever get that chance. Furniture is made to be used, and much of that use spells abuse for the finish. Spilled liquids contribute their share of white rings and dark spots; carelessly handled cigarettes burn ugly holes in the finish; intense summer sun focused by nearby windows dries the finish, leaving it brittle and cracked; dampness and moisture leave once water-clear finishes hazy and cloudy; and the accumulation of dust and dirt dulls the surface. The history of the piece is written into the finish, its time marked by how many near-disasters it has survived.

That, of course, is the main reason that furniture is refinished—sooner or later it gets used up. But a complete refinishing job is not always called for. Much of the damage that finishes suffer in day-to-day use can be corrected. And simple maintenance can keep finishes looking their best for many years.

Restoring Old Finishes

Unless a finish is completely shot, it can sometimes be restored without stripping the piece down to the bare wood and starting over. Finishes that are dull and hazy, mildly water-damaged, or cracked can frequently be brought back to their original appearance. And there is no harm in trying. A failed attempt at restoration can be swiftly corrected with finish remover.

Shellac and some lacquer finishes are the most easily restored because they can be redissolved with solvents. Many of the new finishes, such as the urethanes, are impervious to solvents. The first thing to do is determine if the piece was finished with either shellac or a type of lacquer that will dissolve readily in lacquer thinner. In an inconspicuous place, brush alcohol on a small area. Since alcohol is the solvent for shellac, if the finish begins to soften and smooth out, it is shellac. If the finish is untouched, try a similar approach using lacquer thinner.

RESTORING SHELLAC FINISHES

As shellac finishes age, the resin dries out and loses its elasticity. The surface becomes flaky and granular or develops a pattern of cracks like the skin on an alligator or the dried mud in a desert. This is called an alligatored finish. In addition, moisture will combine with the shellac and produce a surface that is dull and, in extreme cases, white.

But such damage can usually be corrected. First remove all traces of dirt, wax, grease, and other contaminants by washing the piece with a pure soap, such as Ivory flakes, and letting it dry completely. If the piece has been heavily waxed, use a commercial dewaxing solution or wipe the surface with a rag soaked with turpentine. When the surface has dried completely, sand the entire piece with 100-grit sandpaper to cut away the loose, flaky shellac on the surface. Dust the surface thoroughly. Fill any dents or nail holes with lacquer stick.

Then brush or spray the surface with denatured alcohol.

But be extremely careful that the alcohol is fresh and dry. Alcohol will absorb water from the air, and that water will in turn be absorbed into the shellac, leaving a cloudy white surface. It is best to use a new can of alcohol. Also, make absolutely certain that the brush used is completely dry. And work on a day with low humidity.

Spraying will produce the best results, because the finish is not disturbed but is allowed to flow together as it softens. Apply several mist coats of alcohol in succession to allow the shellac to soften but not to run. Then apply a coat of two-pound-cut shellac, wetting the surface thoroughly so that the old and new finish flow together.

If spray equipment is not available, flow the alcohol onto the surface with a good soft brush. Do not be sparing—the object is to saturate the surface completely so that the shellac is dissolved and flows together. Flow on additional alcohol with the tip of the brush until the shellac softens. Ideally, the shellac should be penetrated by the alcohol all the way to the wood. The very dry alcohol will pick up the small amounts of water that are in the finish and carry it away as it evaporates.

Let the piece dry overnight and then sand with 220-grit sandpaper to smooth out any brush marks that may remain and leave a completely smooth surface. Apply at least one coat of two-pound-cut shellac over the entire piece—more if the finish looks as if it should be built up further. Sand and dust between coats, and, finally, rub the finish to the desired gloss. Normally, one or two coats of new shellac should suffice over an existing finish.

RESTORING LACQUER FINISHES

Lacquer finishes can be restored in a similar manner, but not quite as easily. When lacquer goes, it goes. The finish usually breaks down one layer at a time. First a nearly invisible blister appears and then a single coat of lacquer will begin to peel off. The process will continue layer by layer. If the original finish was poorly applied, it may appear that it was finished with layers of plastic film.

Still, that process of disintegration can be arrested. One technique is to follow the same procedure as for shellac but with lacquer thinner. It may work or it may not. The reason is that commercial finishers sometimes mix a variety of stains directly into the lacquer. Various coats may be different colors, shading stains may have been used around the edges. And as the solvent is brushed over the lacquer, those colors will mix. There is, of course, no way to tell without trying, but the result may very well be a finish that is unevenly stained. In that case, the can of finish remover is the next step.

Unless the finish is deeply pitted, an alternative technique is simply to apply new lacquer over the old. This will not completely stop the old finish from breaking down but will slow it considerably. In most instances, it will add two to three years to the life of the finish. Remove all wax and dirt by washing with pure soap and wiping with a dewaxing agent. Then sand the surface thoroughly with 400-grit silicon-carbide paper. Fill any dents, holes, or cracks with lacquer stick. Apply two or more thin coats of lacquer over the old finish. Spray works best because it will not disturb the underlying finish; if a brushing lacquer is used, flow it on with as little brushing as possible. After proper drying, rub and polish to the desired final finish.

RESTORING VARNISH FINISHES

Cracked and alligatored varnish finishes are sometimes restorable as well. Varnish finishes require the use of commercial products called amalgamators since they are not softened readily by a single, easily obtainable solvent. Amalgamators, which also work on lacquer and shellac, can be purchased in good paint stores that specialize in finisher's supplies. They are used in the same way as alcohol to restore shellac finishes.

If the surface is not badly damaged but is simply lusterless and flaky, sanding and applying a coat or two of new varnish will usually bring the finish back. The procedure is the same as for lacquer. Remove dirt and grease, sand with 220-grit sandpaper, repair any small damaged areas with lacquer stick, varnish, and rub to final gloss.

Some Other Alternatives

When finishes are not in seriously bad shape but look dulled with age they can often be greatly improved by rubbing and polishing the surface with pumice and oil. Finely scratched surfaces require sanding first and then may be rubbed and polished. But if too much of the finish is sanded away, they should be given additional coats of finish before rubbing.

Since shellac finishes are so vulnerable to damage from moisture, they are not desirable for pieces that may be exposed to water. A shellacked dining room table, for example, is usually kept covered with pads and a tablecloth during meals. While many fine old tables were finished with shellac back in the days when shellac was the only finish available, it no longer makes much sense. Restoring the water-damaged surface of such a piece is fine—as long as no one is going to eat on it.

The answer in cases where a piece was originally finished with shellac is to restore the shellac finish and then apply a good, water-resistant finish. The beauty of shellac is that it is compatible with almost all other finishes, hence its use as a sealer before finishing. After a shellac finish has been brought back to life with alcohol and sanding, it can be either varnished or lacquered.

The same is not true with other finishes. Applying lacquer over varnish would be a disaster. The finish would lift off and peel away. Lacquer can be applied over varnish only if the surface is first coated with shellac.

Repairing Finishes

There are few things more depressing to someone who has spent hours applying a fine wood finish than to see the surface marred by a carelessly placed glass, dropped object, or forgotten cigarette. But, unfortunately, few finishes are going to make it through very many years before some accident befalls them. With a little effort, however, many types of careless damage can be repaired so that they are practically invisible.

SCRATCHES

Shallow scratches can be repaired in several ways. For objects finished with shellac, simply flow alcohol into the crack. The edges of the crack will dissolve and run together. Lacquer thinner can be used with similar results on lacquered pieces. Alternatively, light brushing with the appropriate solvent will blend the edges of the scratch together. Then rub with pumice and oil. It is a good idea to rub the entire surface on which the repair was made so that the rubbed area will not stand out.

Somewhat deeper scratches should be filled. Scratches in shellac or varnish finishes can be fixed by filling them with new finish. Flow it into the scratch with a fine-tipped brush, then lightly sand the area around the scratch with 400-grit sandpaper, and finally rub the entire surface.

Serious scratches that extend all the way through the finish and into the wood below can be filled with lacquer stick and then rubbed down. Or you can sand them out, then restain wood to match the surrounding area, and build up new finish coats in the repaired area. This, however, is difficult. Unless it is done with skill, the repaired area is not likely to match. The amateur is better off using lacquer stick or refinishing the entire damaged surface.

BURNS

Burns on finished surfaces, such as those left by a burning cigarette or a hot pan or iron carelessly set directly on the wood, can be repaired if the piece got off with shallow damage. But with burns that cover large areas or penetrate deep into the wood, the only alternative is to refinish the entire surface after sanding out the damaged wood and filling in the depression.

If a burn does not extend into the wood, the damaged finish can be sanded away with 100-grit sandpaper, the area smoothed with 220-grit paper, and a couple of coats of the appropriate finish applied to the damaged area. Rubbing the entire surface with pumice and oil will usually hide all signs of repair.

But burns that do not affect the wood are rare. And those that do are a different matter altogether. If the burn covers a relatively small area—not more than 1/2 inch in diameter—the burned wood can be sanded out and the resulting depression filled with lacquer stick. Large, deep burned areas will require filling with a wood filler (use the water-based kind, not premixed resin-based wood doughs). Sand out the damaged wood and fill the depression with wood filler. Allow it to dry overnight, then add another layer to compensate for the shrinkage of the material during the drying. When the filler is completely dry, sand it level with 220-grit sandpaper.

At this stage it is possible to be extremely creative. The filler, of course, lacks the natural markings of wood grain, and some workers—but only those with lots of time and patience—have found ways to fake grain in a convincing manner. Short of faking grain by wiping with different colors of paint, it is possible to cut grain patterns into the filler with a razor blade or utility knife. These should match the pores of the wood surrounding the repair. Going even further, the filler can be stained and sealed, and additional filler mixed with stain can be rubbed into the hand-cut pores.

In most cases, all that is more bother than it is worth. Simply stain the filler to match the surrounding finish, allow the stain to dry, sand lightly with 300-grit sandpaper, and seal the repaired area. Apply at least one coat of finish to the filled area and a final coat over the entire surface. Rub and polish the entire surface.

WATER DAMAGE

White spots and rings that result from leaving wet glassware on many finished surfaces can be removed. They could also have been avoided if the piece had been protected by a coating of wax. In many cases, however, they can be simply polished away with pumice and oil. At least, try that first. If the damage goes too deep to be removed by such fine abrasives, try light sanding with 400-grit silicon-carbide paper. But stick to light sanding—it is always possible that the white area goes all the way through the finish and too much sanding will leave you with a bare spot.

If it looks as if that might be the case, amalgamating the finish with the proper solvent may do the trick. For shellac finishes, for example, use alcohol. Brush solvent onto the whitened area. And take your time. Gradually the whiteness will disappear. Allow the softened area to dry completely, then rub and polish the entire surface.

Dark spots and rings caused by water cannot be corrected without complete refinishing. The darkened wood is caused by water that has penetrated the finish and soaked into the wood. A common culprit for this type of damage is a flowerpot that has been left on a table for a long time. Clay pots are porous and they hold moisture against the wood. The only way those marks can be removed is by bleaching. You must remove the finish, bleach the spot out, bleach the rest of the piece to the same color, then restain and refinish the whole piece.

Maintaining Wood Finishes

Fine finishes can last for decades if they are properly cared for. Just taking a few simple precautions and occasional routine maintenance can make the difference between a finish that becomes more beautiful with age, like a fine old violin, and one that deteriorates into a cracked, lusterless mess. All that is required is to keep the finish clean and protect it from extremes of humidity and temperature.

WAXES AND POLISHES

Almost any furniture finish will profit from a protective coating. Many of the new finishes such as the varnishes and sealers based on urethane or some of the recently developed lacquer formulations are extremely resistant to moisture or heat damage. It has been argued that these finishes do not need waxing. Maybe so, but a coat of wax or occasional polishing certainly will not hurt. It adds an additional line of defense to the finish. And some of the more easily damaged finishes such as shellac positively require waxing to provide a protective barrier to moisture.

Waxes and polishes are available in a confusing variety of forms. There are pastes, liquids, emulsions, and oils. And there are two strongly divided schools of thought between the waxers and the oil polishers. Each, in fact, has a place, although what is ultimately used is usually a matter of personal preference.

WAXING FURNITURE

The most basic form of wax is plain old paste wax. It is also the best wax to use on furniture. The best commercial paste waxes are the ones with the highest percentage of plant waxes such as carnauba or cadelilla. These waxes are extremely hard and provide a durable coating for the wood. They will also buff to a bright glossy surface that will not show fingerprints when it has dried. Other waxes, such as beeswax, are not as hard and will produce a duller surface.

Other forms of waxes are more marketing ploys than anything else. The liquid kinds are simply waxes dissolved in a lot of solvent. The manufacturers claim that they are easier to apply and that the solvent has an added cleaning action. The white emulsion types are mixtures of wax, solvents, water, and sometimes soaps and detergents. The idea is to combine cleaning, polishing, and waxing into a one-step process. Such shortcuts may save time but the most durable and richest-looking wax coats are applied with a good paste wax and lots of elbow grease.

Before waxing, the surface to be coated should be absolutely free of dust and dirt. Any dirt left on the surface will be incorporated into the wax, and eventually the finish will appear to be dark and dull. Dust the surface; if it is very dirty, clean it with a cloth dampened with soapy water or a emulsion-type cleaner. Wipe the piece dry immediately; be especially careful with shellac finishes, which may whiten. Grease can be cleaned off by wiping with a cloth that has been wet with mineral spirits or turpentine.

Make a pad from a soft lint-free cloth such as cheesecloth or an old linen napkin. Apply an even coat of wax by rubbing the pad in a broad circular motion, squeezing the wax onto the surface of the wood. The wax will spread more easily if it is fairly soft. It can be softened by allowing the can to sit in warm water or by thinning the wax with turpentine or mineral spirits. Add a small amount and allow it to dissolve the wax by sitting overnight.

Allow the wax to dry until it is dull. Then buff it with a rough piece of cloth such as burlap or even with a bristle brush of the type used to polish shoes. A final high polish can be produced by rubbing as hard as possible with a soft cloth. If the wax is of good quality and it has been buffed sufficiently, it will not show a print if a finger or thumb is pressed against it.

That probably sounds like an awful lot of effort, but such a coat of wax requires very little maintenance and provides the best protection for a wood finish. When the wax begins to dull, simply dust the surface and buff it back up with a soft cloth. From time to time—it should not be necessary more than once or twice a year—apply a thin layer of fresh wax and repolish the surface. If the finish begins looking dark or dull because of an excessive buildup of wax, which will usually take about 10 years, remove all the wax by wiping with turpentine or mineral spirits and start all over.

POLISHING FURNITURE

Proponents of furniture polishes claim that they provide better protection against moisture than waxes. That is just one of many claims made for polishes and may well be the only one that contains a grain of truth. One common claim, that the polish somehow "feeds" the fibers of the wood, is pure nonsense.

Nonetheless, polishes do serve a useful function. Despite the nearly endless choice of colors and fragrances, furniture polishes are all basically the same thing: mineral oil. And that oil will preserve the elasticity of some finishes, especially varnish. While it will not feed wood, it does penetrate the finish to a certain extent and retards the slow evaporation of volatile components that will eventually leave the finish brittle.

Polishing also cleans dirt off the surface. The drawback is that some polishes also attract dirt more readily than waxes. With some, the only reason a polished piece is shiny is because it is coated with a thin layer of oil. The oil will not harden to a solid film, nor will it evaporate. It remains sticky and collects dust. That, of course, means that the piece will have to be polished frequently to maintain its luster.

Recently, polishes based on silicone have begun appearing on the market. They work fine as polishes—they produce a dry, high-gloss surface. But they also effectively prevent any further refinishing or repair work on the furniture they are used on. *They should never be used on fine finishes or valuable furniture.* The silicone penetrates the finish and even soaks into the wood. Even if the wood is completely stripped, washed, and sanded, the silicone will remain. And no finish will bond to it. Finishes will bead up like water on waxed paper and will lift off like plastic wrap when they have dried.

Temperature and Humidity

Temperature and humidity are the natural enemies of wood and furniture finishes. Prolonged dampness will leave a dull or, at its worst, cloudy or whitened finish. And an environment that is too dry will hasten the evaporation of volatile components from the finish, leaving it brittle and cracked.

Dryness is probably the more serious problem, except in extremely damp climates. It is aggravated by modern heating systems that dry the air excessively during the winter months. That dryness is as bad for furniture as it is for people. The solution is to purchase a home humidifier. Besides helping to prevent the common cold it will keep chairs from becoming wobbly as wood shrinks and will prolong the life of furniture finishes.

High temperatures will cause finishes to dry out and crack. Setting a valuable piece of furniture near a window in the direct sun is subjecting it to serious abuse. Sunlight coming through a window in the summer can heat the surface well above 100° F. That is too close to a laboratory-test method for accelerated aging for comfort. Furthermore, some stains used on furniture will fade in direct sunlight. And the only solution to such fading is to strip the piece completely and start all over. In the summer months, it is a good idea to move valuable furniture away from windows or to keep curtains drawn during the hot part of the day.

Sources of Supplies

Nearly everything needed to finish wood is readily available in local paint stores. The Sherwin-Williams Co., for one, has a multitude of stores from coast to coast that routinely stock a wide assortment of stains, brushes, removers, and other supplies. The paint and hardware departments of both Montgomery Ward & Co. and Sears, Roebuck & Co. are also usually well equipped. In some parts of the country, however, some specialized materials or tools may be difficult to obtain. Fortunately, there are still a few companies that will fill mail orders. And most major manufacturers will be glad to identify local sources of their products. There follow a few selected companies that are sources of both basic and difficult-to-locate materials.

Brookstone Company, Vose Farm Road, Peterborough, N.H. 03458. These "hard to find tool" specialists have a number of things of interest to the furniture finisher. Among their collection of specialized but highly useful tools and gadgets are touch-up finishes for restoring damaged furniture, blocks of hardwood for patches, doweling pins, and even rubber straps for hooking recent acquisitions to the roof of the car. They also sell a good, inexpensive respirator that is a great help in keeping sanding dust out of the nose. They will be glad to send their catalog on request.

Albert Constantine & Son, Inc., 2050 Eastchester Road, Bronx, N.Y. 10461. This company offers a full range of finishers' supplies. It sells everything from finishes to veneers, small pieces of exotic hardwoods for patching, cabinet hardware, and caning supplies. They will send out their complete catalog for $1.00.

192

Craftsmans Wood Service Co., 1735 Cortland Court, Addison, Ill. 60101. Like Constantine's, this company offers just about everything a furniture repairer or finisher would need. It sells finishes, thinners, stains, veneers, hardwoods, repair materials like dowels and cane, tools, and hardware. The company will send a catalog on request.

Period Furniture Hardware Co., 123 Charles Street, Boston, Mass. 12114. This company has an expensive catalog—it's $3.00—but it's well worth the price. Period Hardware specializes in reproductions of antique brass hardware, including everything from fine cabinet hardware to weather vanes and fireplace fixtures. This is the place to go for claw feet, escutcheons, knobs, and latches.

Renovators Supply, Inc., Millers Falls, Mass. 01349. This company started out to supply the home renovation market but has branched into furniture. It has a line of finishes and supplies for caring for furniture as well as a line of antique hardware that includes porcelain, brass, and iron reproductions at reasonable prices. The company sells its catalog for $2.00 but will refund that amount against a purchase. It will also answer telephone inquiries at (413) 659-3542.

H. L. Wild, 510 East Eleventh Street, New York, N.Y. 10009. This venerable family-run company supplies fine woods and specialized woodworking tools to makers of furniture and stringed musical instruments. They sell a complete range of veneers and offer exotic hardwoods planed to exact dimensions. In addition, Wild sells precut decorative pieces of veneer and mother of pearl for marquetry and decorating musical instruments. Veneer saws, patch cutters, and fine woodcarving tools are also available. They will send a copy of their catalog for $1.50.

Index